NEW AND EXPANDED VERSION OF

FAITH-SHARING:
DYNAMIC CHRISTIAN
WITNESSING BY INVITATION

H. EDDIE FOX
GEORGE E. MORRIS

Prepared under the Direction of the World Methodist Council

DISCIPLESHIP RESOURCES

P.O. BOX 340003 • NASHVILLE, TN 37203-0003
www.discipleshipresources.org

WORLD EVANGELISM LIBRARY

A World Evangelism Library has been established by the World Evangelism Committee of the World Methodist Council. From time to time, books will be published to explore and explain the meaning of evangelism. Behind the books that are added to the Library will be scholarly research and actual experience in the practice of evangelism. Each book will be a responsible expression of evangelical Christianity, discussing issues of vital concern to every Christian and the whole church. The Library aims to enlarge the resources of evangelism for every part of the church of Jesus Christ. The first five books of the Library are

1. *The Mystery and Meaning of Christian Conversion,* by George E. Morris (Discipleship Resources, 1981).
2. *Standing Up to Preach: The Art of Evangelical Preaching,* by Alan Walker (Discipleship Resources, 1983).
3. *Faith-Sharing: Dynamic Christian Witnessing by Invitation,* by George E. Morris and H. Eddie Fox (Discipleship Resources, 1986; revised edition, 1996).
4. *Connecting With the Spirit of Christ,* by Christopher C. Walker (Discipleship Resources, 1988).
5. *Let the Redeemed of the Lord SAY SO!* by H. Eddie Fox and George E. Morris (Abingdon Press, 1991).

Reprinted 2002, 2000, 1998

Images © 1996 PhotoDisc, Inc.

ISBN: 0-88177-158-9

Library of Congress Catalog Card No. 96-84197

DR158

*"I pray that the sharing of
your faith may become effective
when you perceive all the good
that we may do for Christ."*

PHILEMON 6 (NRSV)

In loving memory of
HARRY DENMAN

whose worldwide ministry was a demonstration
of committed and compassionate

Faith-Sharing

Contents

Foreword

I am delighted that George Morris and Eddie Fox are providing us a "revised and expanded version" of *Faith-Sharing*. The reception and use of the book is proof that it is a much-needed and timely resource, welcomed by those who long for a recovery of the vital personal evangelism that faith-sharing can bring to the church. It is not often that theory and practice are brought together in such balance. Lay people will find here inspiration and motivation for their calling as Christians to spread the gospel. They will also find the practical resources to equip them for the task.

Since the first edition of this book, almost earthshaking things have happened. The opening of the former Soviet Union and the Eastern Bloc has given the church challenging evangelistic opportunity. George Morris and Eddie Fox have made a thrilling response to that challenge. Through World Evangelism of the World Methodist Council, a unique program called "Connecting Congregations" has come to be. These new "Connecting Congregations" are being developed on every continent, and they are led by indigenous leaders trained by the World Methodist Evangelism Institute in faith-sharing theology and practice. During the last decade these faith-sharing principles have been taught by Morris and Fox in countries on every continent.

The first edition of *Faith-Sharing* has been translated into several languages, and more than 100,000 copies have been sold in the English edition. In addition, since the release of the first edition, the authors have developed two major resources for use in the training of pastors and lay persons: *The Faith-Sharing New Testament* and the Faith-Sharing Video. Dr. Fox guides the program of World Evangelism and Dr. Morris is the senior professor of the World Methodist Evangelism Institute. These men "practice what they preach."

The revised and expanded edition of this book will be a great tool for pastors and others who have the responsibility of recruiting and training persons for the evangelistic task. Many of us have longed for adequate assistance in training others in faith-sharing. The task-oriented principles and guidelines of this book provide us the "handles" to do that training.

I am delighted that this is not just a how-to book, nor is it just a challenging call. It is rooted in that basic Christian concern for persons. We must share the faith, not for the sake of the church but for the sake of the persons with whom we share. To be sure, the writers are committed to church growth, and this is a significant resource for that cause. Their commitment to church growth is not reflexive institutional pride, but is rooted in the passion for sharing the gospel, that persons may become the recipients of the grace of God which alone brings salvation and wholeness.

These writers sense their roots in a practical Christianity which knows everyday life is the arena for living discipleship, and they see every Christian as a "called" person who may participate in God's idea of a "kingdom of priests"—a kingdom of faith-sharers.

I don't know two people more equipped for the writing of such a book. George Morris and Eddie Fox have distinguished themselves in the field of evangelism and faith-sharing. By study and experience, they are authorities in the theology and practice of witnessing. I chair the World Evangelism Committee of the World Methodist Council. George Morris and Eddie Fox are significant leaders in world evangelism, and I look forward to a future in which I will continue to be yoked with them in a task that demands more than we can ever give, but is called for and undergirded by the One to whom the kingdoms of this world will one day bow down.

Theology is here—solidly Christian and popularly written. Instruction is here—clear and practical. Challenge is here—in the spirit of Him who gave the command: "Go into all the world and preach the gospel." Concern is here—"that the world may believe," Christians must share.

I write this Foreword with the prayer that those who read it will become "doers of the Word."

MAXIE D. DUNNAM
President, Asbury Theological Seminary

Acknowledgments

The writers are grateful to several authors and publishers for permission to quote from their works. We are especially grateful to all those whose ideas may have slipped into our own consciousness and surfaced here as our own. Having been informed by so many teachers, authors, colleagues, and friends, it would be impossible to acknowledge all of them.

A special word of thanks is rendered to those numerous pastors and laypersons from across the United States and around the world with whom we have shared, developed, and tested the materials contained in this book. We have attempted to respond to every suggestion. This process of "field-testing" has been enriching for the authors and, we believe, will greatly enhance the value of this book.

Chapters 3, 6, and 7 were originally delivered as the 1986 Denman Lectures. We are grateful to the Foundation on Evangelism for the sponsorship of these lectures and trust that the inclusion of these chapters will appropriately honor Harry Denman, to whom the entire book is dedicated. Chapter 2 originally appeared in *Ministry and Mission*, edited by Barbara Brown Taylor. Throughout the book, we have worked together and have contributed ideas to all areas. We have identified individual experiences as such.

Genuine appreciation is expressed to Julia D'Andrea, Shirley Clement, Theresa Santillan, Sharon Wells, Mary Hall, and Ann Robinson for their assistance in preparing the manuscript. We are particularly grateful to Shirley Clement for contributing the Reflection-Action exercises at the conclusion of each chapter. Moreover, we would be remiss if we failed to acknowledge our deepest gratitude for the encouragement, support, and modeling of *Faith-Sharing* on the part of our wives, Mary Nell Fox and Barbara Morris.

At the end of each chapter there are suggestions for reflection and action. These ideas can be used as individual as well as group experiences. Several options are included for each chapter. Perhaps you would like to select those options which would be most helpful.

We have attempted to follow the leadership of the Holy Spirit in the writing of this book. However, where we have misread the signals, we assume complete responsibility. It is our sincere prayer that the reader will experience these materials as practical help which is theologically and biblically grounded. We live in the hope that God will use this material to multiply the numbers of Christian faith-sharers throughout the world.

GEORGE E. MORRIS
Dan and Lil Hankey
Senior Professor;
World Methodist
Evangelism Institute

H. EDDIE FOX
World Director of World Evangelism
World Methodist Council;
Executive Director
World Methodist Evangelism Institute

Faith-Sharing Is God's Idea

A t the home of a deputy ambassador in a South American country 150 people gathered. In the crowd were English-speaking persons who had recently moved to the city. Most were employees of government or multinational corporations. In addition, there were twenty-five clergy from Central and South America. These clergy were attending a conference in the city, and they had come to the reception to hear the story of a missionary and his ministry among a tribe of people in a very remote area. As usual, slides were shown and stories were told.

The missionary told how, as a ten-year-old lad, he came with his father who was the first Christian missionary. He grew up among the tribe and learned the language of the people. After finishing school in the United States, he returned as a missionary. For more than twenty years he labored to translate the New Testament into the language of the people.

Following the missionary's presentation he asked if there were any questions. "Any tigers out there?" "Oh, yes, there are tigers out there! I remember the first time I spent the night out in the jungle in a bamboo hammock. I heard a noise. I asked my guide, 'What's that?' 'Oh, just a tiger; go back to sleep,' he answered. Well, you don't go back to sleep when it's just a tiger!"

The next question was about menu and diet. All of the questions were similar until one of the people, not in the clergy group, stood to ask his question. "Sir, would you please tell me why these people should be Christian? Why should you tell them about your God? What right do you have to change them?" The meeting became quiet—very quiet.

This experience of one of the authors[1] raises a question in the minds of many people in our society. It is a basic question: *Why?* Many people, both inside and outside the church, are asking this question: Why should we share Christian faith with others?

Many images are raised by this question. Some of us envision enlightened people bringing their religion to the heathen. This image raises real tension in the minds of many people. Even inside the church the question is raised: "Why share faith? Don't you know that religion is a private affair? After all, we don't want to manipulate people. We are here, and if people want Christian faith, they will come to the church just like they go to the grocery store." Now we may not state it so forthrightly, but by our actions and attitudes we reveal the depth of our uncertainty: Why share faith?

For more than two decades, the authors have met with thousands of Christians from all around the world who are most reluctant to share their faith with others. Today the church is in a mission situation just as it was in the days of the apostles. As Loren Mead reminds us, "The early church was conscious of itself as a faithful people surrounded by a hostile environment to which each member was called to witness to God's love in Christ."[2] If one wonders what it would have been like to live in the New Testament time, then today one can sing "Home Sweet Home." We live in a culture as alien to the Christian faith as was the culture into which the Christian faith was born.

In this mission situation persons who are outside the fellowship of the Christian church tend to see the church as a "private institution." That is, people who pass by our church buildings do not see them as public buildings. People who are outside will not come in without an invitation. Therefore, the need for committed, well-trained faith-sharers is greater than ever.

The reality is that multitudes of Christians are very reluctant faith-sharers. The desire to multiply the number of faith-sharers has been a consuming passion of ours for many years—because, through the ministry of faith-sharing, persons are introduced to the good news of Christ Jesus!

If we are to be encouraged and sustained in this ministry of faith-sharing, we must begin with the most fundamental question: Why share faith?

This question is so significant that we will address it in two chapters. In this chapter we will deal with two fundamentals in Bible teaching: Faith-sharing is grounded in the nature of God, and it is in response to the need of humanity.

THE SEEKING GOD

First, faith-sharing is God's idea; God started the whole process. For the Christian, the story of God's reach for humanity is centered in the person of Jesus Christ. Of course, there are many chapters to this story, but the center of the compass for the Christian is the event of God in Jesus Christ. From this perspective we view and hear the whole story.

God is a seeking God whose nature is shown in creation and in the divine intention to recreate a new humanity after people turned away in disobedience and sin. The story is one of God reaching out for a relationship of wholeness with all creation. God creates out of nothing, establishes order in the midst of chaos, and declares creation as good.

God creates male and female and declares them "very good." The Creator establishes order in creation, and humankind created in the image of God is given the dignity, freedom, and grace to respond to the invitation of God to participate in the fullness of creation.

God's loving outreach is seen not only in God's creative activity but also in God's continuing sustaining providence in the world. God is caring and is actively involved in human history. It is the unswerving purpose of God to establish the kingdom on earth as it is in heaven. This is the central theme of the Bible. God persists toward the ultimate fulfillment of this plan for creation.

In the midst of our disobedience, self-will, and rejection of divine initiative, God broods over creation. God reaches out to redeem and restore a relationship with a proud, broken, and sinful humanity. From the beginning of creation, the quest for relationship is primarily a divine quest. God is the seeker, the pursuer, the searcher. Thus, salvation is God's idea.

In the gospel story, note how many people "find" the Lord while running away from God. The question asked of Adam and Eve is asked of all humanity: "Where are you?" The gospel story is a story of God's seeking activity. Moreover, God is seen as the liberator who sets people free. Before even one commandment is given in the decalogue, God declares, "I . . . brought you out of the land of Egypt" (Exod. 20:1-2, NRSV). The Ten Commandments must be seen in this light. We do not keep the commandments in order to get God to liberate us; the Commandments are an expression of obedience to a God who already has acted to set us free.

Consider the story of Jonah. He was a very reluctant witness. He was not a candidate as a "volunteer in mission." In fact, he resisted strongly the call of God to be a witness for God to the people in Nineveh. Sometimes we think Jonah may have been the first Methodist, for he was a most reluctant missionary. Moreover, we have to add, there was no pulpit committee in Nineveh either. The citizens of Nineveh did not hold a council meeting and call for a missionary. Clearly, the idea that the people should hear and know God is rooted in the very nature of God.

God acts redemptively in human history. Paul Scherer writes, "From start to finish the biblical writers are concerned first and foremost with the mighty saving acts of God. The historian records them, the prophets proclaim them, and the Psalmists celebrate them."[3]

The Old Testament prophets pointed toward the coming day when God would act to make possible this new relationship of wholeness between Creator and creation. Jeremiah looked toward the time when the Lord would make a new covenant:

> I will set my law within them and write it on their hearts;
> I will become their God and they shall become my people
> (Jer. 31:33, NEB).

Isaiah expected the arrival of a Messiah, who would establish a righteous reign:

> For unto us a child is born, unto us a son is given: and the *government* shall be upon his shoulder . . . Of the increase of his government and peace there shall be no end, upon the throne of David, and upon his kingdom, to order it, and to establish it with judgment and with justice from henceforth even forever. The zeal of the Lord of hosts will perform this (Isa. 9:6-7, KJV).

Clearly, this is all the Lord's doing. God takes the initiative in self-disclosure and revelation. Therefore, when Jesus was born there was a community of people who fully anticipated such action.

The coming of Jesus was the ultimate unique declaration of God's initiative to establish a relationship of wholeness with all creation. God arranged a heavenly choir to announce the good news to the ordinary people of the day, the shepherds. And even the heavens declared this in-breaking word to the wise men of that time. The birth, life, death, and resurrection of Jesus was the climax of God's redemptive plan. These powerful events were to be announced to the whole world (Luke 24:45-49). Therefore, a fundamental truth for the Christian is that the "Word became flesh; he came to dwell among us" (John 1:14, NEB).

Jesus used many images that point to the seeking nature of God. He told of a shepherd who had one hundred sheep, and one became lost. The shepherd left the ninety-nine and went looking for the lost sheep until he *found* it. When he found the lost sheep, the rejoicing began. He also told of a woman who had ten silver coins and lost one. She lit a lamp, swept the house, moved the furniture, and looked carefully everywhere until she *found* it. Upon finding it, the rejoicing began.

Then Jesus told the story of a boy who left his father's home to go into a far country. The boy—after failure, loss, hunger, and despair—came to his senses and started for his father's house. Notice the image of God in this parable. Jesus said that while the son was still a "long way off" *his father saw him*. The father *ran* to meet the son. The father *hugged*, and the father *kissed* the son. The son's response to his father's action was one of confession and repentance. Then the celebration began, because a son who was dead had come back to life—a son who was lost had been found! But this is not the end of the story.

The older brother was working in the field. On his way home he heard music and dancing. He was hurt and angry and refused to join the party. The father came out and pleaded with his son, but he refused to take part in the celebration. This self-righteous, jealous older brother was upset that the father would give such a party for a son who had squandered his inheritance. But miracle of all miracles, the father reached out to his oldest son and declared, "You are always with me and all that is mine is yours" (Luke 15:31, NRSV).

When one hears or reads this story, one is left with a haunting question: "Did the older brother finally come into the party?" We do not know, but when the story closes, the father is still outside. God is a gracious, seeking, inviting God.

We share faith with others because we worship the God whose nature is one of self-disclosure. Faith-sharing does not start with us but with God. It is God's idea. We see this truth in John Newton's "Amazing Grace," which declares, "I once was lost, but now *am found*."[4] Moreover, Francis Thompson sees God as the pursuing "Hound of Heaven."[5] God looks for us long before we ever look for God.

Indeed, God's love and mercy have followed us all the days of our lives. The Lord goes with us through green fields, beside still waters, and through valleys of deepest darkness. Therefore, any consideration of faith-sharing must be rooted in an understanding of the living God who is disclosed as Immanuel, "God with us."

Thus far, we have seen how God is moving toward us, seeking us, calling us, and enabling us to come to new life. We have seen that it is God who takes the initiative to establish a new covenant and a relationship of wholeness with all of creation. **Faith-sharing is God's idea.**

HUMANITY NEEDS CHRISTIAN FAITH

We also share Christian faith because people need Christian faith. The human race, in an act of self-will, turns away from God in disobedience. This broken relationship results in alienation and estrangement. Humanity in its pride and disobedience attempts to hide from God but discovers the ultimate futility of such an attempt. To reject the divine invitation of God is to have wholeness shattered.

Sin (a broken relationship with God) is a tragic consequence of our self-will and disobedience. The fruit of our turning away from God is to be captive to our own distorted vision of ourselves, others, and the world. This separation from God has tragic consequences for all of humanity. We are in bondage together. Leander Keck reminds us that "sin is no mere kink in the soul."[6]

By sin we mean both the breaking of our relationship with God and the specific acts which violate the will of God and the nature of humankind. The human situation is that of a debtor. People are born, so to speak, with mortgages on their hands. They are born into a family with an enormous pile of overdue bills, and to this stack of accounts each person adds his or her own new debts.

We are called, then, to share faith because of human need and human worth. Persons are of great value and worth because they are created in the image of God and pronounced good. In fact, God declared that they are "very good." One of the authors' experiences with his children confirms this important affirmation.[7] For an elementary school science project one of his twin sons decided he would plot the stars of the heavens. He made a "star gazer" and plotted the apparent movement of the Ursa Major (Big Dipper) around the Polaris (North Star).

It was a cold night for star plotting, and father and son were outside at 8:00, 10:00, and midnight. The father was freezing, but the son was excited! He noted that the stars were exactly where they were supposed to be. He finally declared, "Dad, it is all neat and in order, isn't it?" Dad replied with feeling, "Son, it sure is, and we know who made it that way. And we know that the same God made us." This is the story of the biblical revelation. God declares the worth of creation, including the great value of humanity.

However, the great tragedy in the gospel story is that the invitation to participate in the fullness of creation is rejected. Sin is turning away from God, away from neighbors, and creation, and turning inward upon the self. Because the human race is alienated from God, it attempts to hide from God and desperately gropes in darkness.

In our society it is not difficult to see the discrepancy between God's vision and reality. Not only in human hearts but also in the world's principalities and powers there is the enslavement of people (Eph. 6:12). A few years ago there was a popular book entitled, *I'm OK, You're OK.* It was very helpful to many people in regard to their self-understanding and self-esteem. But some have asked, "If I'm OK and you're OK, then who in the world is causing all the trouble?"

When we look at the atrocities which some people commit against others, and when we see how unjust systems enslave people, we are keenly aware of the need for raw human nature to be changed through Christian conversion. There is that which needs to be put right with the Creator. Wesley spoke of the "bent to sinning"—a radical flaw which calls for a redemptive power from beyond ourselves.

This radical flaw—sin—results in bondage unto death. It is like a spreading malignant disease which destroys and corrupts the whole creation. All are infected by this spiritual sickness. The scripture makes clear the universality of sin:

> All, both Jews and Greek are under the power of sin. There is no one who is righteous, not even one; there is no one who has understanding, there is no one who seeks God. All have turned aside . . . (Rom. 3:9-12a, NRSV).

John Wesley describes the human situation as utterly destitute. The image of God is so disfigured and distorted that humans are totally incapable of redeeming themselves. This bondage is so complete and sin is so radically rooted in human nature that to break its power we need a Savior. Jesus Christ is the Savior of the world. This is the incredible good news of the faith-sharer: God has acted in the birth, life, death, and resurrection of Jesus Christ to make possible our being put right (reconciled) to God. Through Christ the entire human race is given the possibility of redemption through the graciousness of God.

GOD'S NATURE

Thus far we have outlined two basic reasons for sharing our Christian faith with others: (1) The good news of a seeking God, and (2) the great need and potential of humanity. The good news is that God has acted uniquely and ultimately in the person of Jesus Christ and through this revelation has offered the gift of forgiveness and new life to those who respond in repentance and faith. This is a message worth sharing!

In conclusion, if we are to engage in sharing faith normally and naturally, we must be clear in our understanding of God. What we believe about God makes a difference in our response to God and the way we live and share faith with others. Our behavior is fundamentally conditioned by our understanding of the nature of God.

In James Michener's book, *The Source*, we have a powerful illustration of how our understanding of God influences our actions. The book is about a team of archeologists excavating an ancient city in the Holy Land. In ancient days when a city was destroyed by fire or war, the people did not go ten miles away to build another. They built the new city upon the rubble of the old. Through hundreds of years, as a result of this process, a huge mound called a *tel* would develop. Thus, we derive names such as Tel Aviv. Archeologists, by peeling back layer after layer and examining the artifacts, can interpret what life was like during different eras of history. This is the literary device which Michener uses in his book.

There is a scene in the book depicting what life was like in that region long before the rise of the Hebrew religion and its faith in the one true God. The author paints a graphic picture of a young woman standing in the doorway of her house, watching as her husband takes their first-born child to the temple to be offered as a human sacrifice to a pagan fertility god. This was thought to be an act of worship. In this ancient religion it was believed that in order to assure fertility in the family and on the farm, the first-born child had to be sacrificed.

The mother's heart is breaking. All during her pregnancy, she has tried to prepare herself for this terrible moment, but nothing could prepare her for such pain and sorrow. Tears are streaming down her cheeks.

Later, we see this same woman standing in her doorway. Only this time she watches as her husband goes to the temple to consort with temple prostitutes. This too was thought to be an act of worship, assuring fertility in the family and on the farm. Tears are streaming down her cheeks as she points to her husband and says, "If he had had a different god, he would have been a different man." Our understanding of the nature of God makes a great deal of difference.

The God revealed in Jesus Christ is holy, great, good, and gracious. It is in the living God of grace and glory that faith-sharing is rooted. Faith-sharing is God's idea. In the next chapter we will discover that we share faith because of God's grace and our gratitude.

REFLECT AND ACT

1. How would you answer the question to the missionary in South America? Why should you tell people about God? Why should we share Christian faith with others?

2. How do you respond to the comment that religion is a private affair?

3. Were you ever running away from God or hiding? What were you running or hiding from? What were the moments when you were "found" by God? How did you feel in being found? Did you want to rejoice? How did you express that joy? Has anyone else ever shared that experience with you? What parts of their story related to the above questions do you remember?

4. What beliefs about the nature of God affect your living? Reflect on your actions in relationships and your reactions to stories of events in the world in the last two days. How has your belief in the nature of God affected your response?

5. In this chapter, sin is defined as a broken relationship with God, a consequence of humankind's self-will and disobedience. The fruit of our turning away from God is to be captive, in bondage, to our own distorted vision of ourselves, others, and the world. What areas of your own life are still in bondage and in need of healing and new life?

6.

Scripture	Story	Life Situation
Gen. 2:18–3:24	Adam and Eve hiding from God	
1 Kings 18:1–19:18	Elijah hiding from Jezebel and God	
Luke 15:11-32	A younger son who runs away	
Luke 15:11-32	An older son who stays outside	

What are the life conditions and situations in each of these passages? Are there any similarities to situations in life today? Any to your own life?

2
Love: The Motive for Faith-Sharing

arold DeWolf, former professor of systematic theology at both
Boston and Wesley Schools of Theology, once said, "The New
Testament church engaged in evangelism as naturally and normally as a robin sings or a happy child plays."[1] In making this comment DeWolf was trying to offset the popular misconception that evangelizing is a special ministry that must be done by special people at special times and in special ways, rather than through the natural, normal
ministry of the church.

It is the recovery of this natural aspect of faith-sharing that is receiving much of the energy and creativity of leaders in today's church.
These leaders dream of a church which will view its evangelizing mandate not as a special chore, but as the normal, faithful, day-by-day
manifestation of the church's authentic life.

However, we are convinced that faith-sharing will not become a natural, normal part of the life of the church until the motives for it are
clarified. To multitudes of laity and clergy, these motives are not clear,
and this confusion impedes the sharing of faith. Therefore, at the beginning of this chapter we affirm the following: (1) Our faith-sharing falls
into disrepute without genuine attention concerning our motives; (2)
much that served as powerful motivation in times past is no longer adequate for today; (3) contemporary faith-sharing must find a legitimate
theological motive.

First, let us look at some of the grounds for faith-sharing in the past
and why these motives are questionable today.

SOME QUESTIONABLE MOTIVES

Alan Walker is right in his observation that the driving motive of much eighteenth- and nineteenth-century evangelism was that of *preserving souls*.[2] With a vivid belief in the substantive reality of heaven and hell, Christian evangelists sought to rescue people from eternal punishment and open for them the door of heaven before it was everlastingly too late.

We need to question this approach. Are these motives credible? Are fear of death and doom, and hope of reward worthy motives for belief? Given the fact that the lengthening life span is pushing death further and further into the future, is death the threat it once was? You see, it is one thing to use death and eternal damnation as a motivational prod when one's listeners are very death-conscious. It is something else to be confronted with a life-conscious "boomer" or "buster" generation whose fundamental question is not, "Is there life after death?" but, "Is there life after birth?"

However, this shifting of consciousness presents the church with a marvelous opportunity, because the Christian gospel is a gospel of eternal life which upholds the sanctity of life. In the second century Bishop Irenaeus of Lyons, our first theologian, said "God's glory is man/woman alive!"[3]

Moreover, Martin Luther and John Wesley questioned the use of fear as a motive. Luther insisted that fear causes us to hate the cause of fear:

> And this is the only way to achieve a true conversion, namely through love and kindness. For he who is converted through threats and terror is never truly converted as long as he retains that form of conversion. For fear makes him hate his conversion. But he who is converted by love is completely burned up against himself and is far more angry with himself than anyone else can be with him, and he is totally displeased with himself.[4]

John Wesley wrote, "It cannot be that they should long obey God from fear who are deaf to the motives of love."[5]

In addition, we are skeptical about motivation rooted in the hope of reward. It tends to play into the hands of our contemporary consumer mentality, our tendency to ask, "What's in it for me?" Instead of addressing itself to our desperate needs, it tends to pander to our selfish wants. In the language of Soren Kierkegaard, this is a form of "double-mindedness."[6] In his book *Purity of Heart*, Kierkegaard contends that when a person wills the good for the sake of reward, he or she does not will one thing but two. To will the good for the sake of reward is double-mindedness. So we are dubious of those who wonder "what's in it for me?" Though some still appeal to fear and reward motives, we are convinced that they are inadequate by their very nature.

A popular motive in our generation has been that of *preserving the institution*. Shortly after receiving an appointment to a small congregation, a new pastor[7] was approached by one of the church leaders: "You ought to visit a certain lieutenant colonel who has moved into our community. You had better get over there and get him before the Baptists interfere. If we could enlist him in our church, he surely would help us with the budget!" Obviously, the leader had little concern for the person. The real concern was the institution and its preservation.

For some, preserving the institution may become the basic focus of faith-sharing. The more threatened the institution becomes, the more defensive it is, and the more its leaders tend to recruit in order to preserve it. Realizing that people cannot be coerced into membership, leaders are tempted to seduce them to join. Thus, the church tries to "pretty itself up" with all sorts of attractive accoutrements in order to present a competitive image which draws people to itself. The church becomes a seducer rather than a converter, leading to a style of cultural accommodation that tends to abandon the radical claims of the gospel.

There are always subtle temptations involved in the attempt to make the Christian faith attractive so it will "sell." The temptation is ever present to silence the absolute claim of God's Lordship. Where this is done, the gospel loses its salt and becomes sugary.

This institutional motivation has helped to create what we call the "edifice complex." This complex is widespread to the extent that most of our people think "building" when they hear "church." If a visitor from Mars were to come to you at ten o'clock on Tuesday morning and ask, "Where is your church?" how would you reply? Would it occur to you to say, "Some of the church are in the public schools, some in the factories and offices, some in their homes"?

Many lay people who work on visitation teams tell us that they see themselves as going forth to represent the church. It would never occur to many of them that they *are* the church going forth! One of the great tasks in equipping for faith-sharing is that of enabling people to re-image the church, that is, to think "people" when they hear "church."

Another popular motive for faith-sharing in Europe and the United States has been the *expansion and preservation of our national life*. The expansionist motive was best illustrated in the doctrine of "manifest destiny." Protestant leaders combined faith in God with faith in their own culture's virtues. Suddenly, Protestantism was inspired with the desire to convert people, in order to spread Anglo-Saxon civilization, to expand and conquer. First the British, then North Americans, spoke of themselves as the "New Israel" which had received the heathen for an inheritance. The idea of the expanding empire became the equivalent of the growth of the kingdom of God. Thus, some missionary work was a blending of evangelization and westernization.

Once the expansionist period of "manifest destiny" had run its course, another motive set in—using evangelism as a means of preserving our gains against outside attacks. Thus, a driving force of much so-called evangelism of our recent past has been preserving our national character against the attacks of communists, secular humanists, and non-Christian religions. This has tended to produce a defensive posture which mistakes nationalistic propaganda for the good news of the gospel.

LEGITIMATE MOTIVATION

If these motives are questionable, what would constitute legitimate motivation for faith-sharing? The answer lies in three affirmations: (1) Faith-sharing is founded in God's love; (2) it fulfills the Great Commission; and (3) it focuses on total redemption.

FAITH-SHARING IS FOUNDED IN GOD'S LOVE

The two words, *God's love*, are crucial to our understanding. The first affirms that the responsibility for faith-sharing ministries is rooted in the very nature of God. Faith-sharing is necessary because of *who* God is. Accordingly, faith-sharing has its origin in the nature of our Triune God. Our Creator God is a living, loving, willing, acting Spirit—a personal God (Eph. 1: 1-11; Exod. 3:14). As we have seen in the previous chapter, from the creation and fall, and throughout history, God has always been in search of lost humans.

God is not only a seeking God; God is a sending God. Both of these emphases are caught up in the important New Testament word *mission*. The word *mission* comes from the Latin *mittere*, which is a translation of two Greek words, *pempo* and *apostello*. All of these words have to do with "sending." They rest on four assumptions: (1) There is Someone who sends—God; (2) there is that which God sends—God's message—which is actually a communication of God's self; (3) there is the messenger; and (4) there is the recipient.

As you can see, from beginning to end this is a person-to-person concept. A person on one end is reaching out to persons at the other end. This is just another way of saying that faith-sharing begins in God. It is a part of God's nature and will. Therefore, we share in God's mission. Our mission is valid only as it is a participation in the mission of God. The shorthand for this is the Latin phrase *missio Dei*. It means that God is a missionary God, whose heart feels and longs and loves, a God who seeks us down the corridors of time. The living God comes into the broken order of our lives to dwell with us in person-to-person relationships.

Next, the word *mission* also tells us that God is a sending God. This theme winds its way through the biblical text. John R. W. Stott outlines this theme.[8] God sent Abraham from his country and kindred into the great unknown, promising to bless him and to bless the world through him. God sent Joseph into Egypt, overcoming his brothers' cruelty, in order to preserve a remnant on earth. God sent Moses to an oppressed people in Egypt with the good news of liberation. God sent a continuous succession of prophets with words of warning and promise. Then, at last when the time had fully come, God sent forth the Son, and later, on the day of Pentecost, the Spirit.

Now the Son sends as he himself was sent. Jesus said, "As the Father sent me, so I send you" (John 20:21, NEB). During his public ministry Jesus sent out first the apostles and then the seventy as a kind of extension of his own preaching, teaching, and healing. Then after his death and resurrection, Christ widened the scope of the mission to include all who call him Lord.

In summary, the church is forever being challenged to become the instrument of God's sending and seeking. It must structure itself so as to serve its missionary God, and it must reject whatever leads only to its own security and self-aggrandizement. Faith-sharing is founded in God. If you ask us, "Why do you share faith?" we reply, "Because we are servants of the living God." But there is more.

Faith-sharing is founded in the *love* of God. Since it is God's love we are considering, and since we believe that God is love, it is actually impossible to separate these two key words. Yet, for the moment, let us focus on the *love* side of the equation.

With the advent of Jesus Christ nearly two thousand years ago, the Greek Christians were faced with a dilemma. Jesus was both the exemplar and the exponent of a love that was so different that the Greeks did not have a word to express it. So they dipped back into their history, resurrected an old word that was not in vogue—*agape*—and poured new meaning and content into it. What does this word mean?

Agape is a love shown by the desire to *help* the object of its devotion rather than to *possess* it. Here we would like to share with you four points that have been informing and shaping our understanding of what it means to share faith. These principles are written so indelibly upon our hearts that we cannot escape their pressure for very long.

1. To grasp the meaning of *agape* one must first realize that it is **not a natural endowment**. The human being does not possess this love naturally. It is not something with which we are born. If it were a natural part of us, then all that would be necessary would be to get out the bellows and stoke it up a bit. It would be appropriate to set the jaw, grit the teeth, squint the eye, and say, "I'm going to have *agape* if it kills me!" But *agape* is not a part of our natural endowment. We cannot conjure it up. There is only one way to experience *agape*, and that is to receive it as a gift.

2. We must realize that *agape* is a **gift from God**. This is best presented in the familiar verse John 3:16: "God so loved the world that he gave . . ." (NEB). There is no way to earn this love, to deserve it. If we possess it at all, we possess it as a gift. It is God's love in us—so in a real sense we have no claim on it. Because it is God's love in us, we have nothing of which to boast. Our only legitimate response is one of grateful stewardship. We become stewards of God's love in us.

3. *Agape* of its very nature **makes both the giver and the recipient vulnerable**. In pouring out love upon us, God takes an awesome risk. God risks the possibility that people will not respond to love, and many do not. However, this does not deter God. God does not say, "Because all people do not respond to my love, I shall refuse to give my love to anyone." No! God gives the gift whether we receive it or not. This is what we mean when we talk about the vulnerability of God. Nowhere is this seen more clearly than on the cross.

    But, suppose we respond to the gift of God's love? Suppose we say *yes* to God's love? In that moment we make ourselves vulnerable. If we open our lives and receive God's love, there is only one way that we can express our overwhelming gratitude for such an unmerited gift—by turning that love loose upon others. In so doing we find ourselves sharing in the vulnerability of God. By allowing God to love others through us, we also find ourselves sharing the pain of rejection and the joy of acceptance. Christian discipleship is sharing the vulnerability of God. Thus, we find ourselves loving the unlovable—even loving those whom we do not particularly like.

4. *Agape* is seated more in the active will than in the emotions. Did you ever wonder why the Bible commands love? It does not say, "Love one another if you feel like it," or "if you're going to get something out of it," or "if you're going to be loved back in return," or "if it's convenient for you." No! The Bible says, "Love one another." That is the reason *agape* is a verb. It means that we take action for the sake of the other even when we do not feel like it.

   It also means that we are willing to take responsibility for our actions. That is, we know we might take the wrong action, but we are willing to risk error for the sake of sharing God's love. Our lives are so filled with gratitude for the gift of God's love that we are constrained to love others (2 Cor. 5:14).

Thus, the primary motive for faith-sharing and all discipleship is founded in God's love. Michael Green is correct when he insists that the main motive for the faith-sharing of the early Christians was a theological one, not an institutional one. They shared faith because of the overwhelming experience of the love of God in Christ Jesus.[9]

The disciples had no difficulty asking the people to say *yes* to the living God who had already said *yes* to them. They responded to the gospel in loving gratitude, and they shared the gospel with boldness and confidence (2 Cor. 5:14). The living Christ encountering them in the gospel was the normative thing. Thus, for them, the gospel of Jesus Christ was utterly normative.

IMPLICATIONS FOR FAITH-SHARING

What would it imply if we acknowledged that faith-sharing is God's idea and love the primary motive? Perhaps these seven things:

1. We would give first priority to the gospel, not to the institutional church. Granted, the institutional church is a part of the gospel, a part of what God has done for the salvation of the world. But the institutional church is *only* a part.

2. Therefore, instead of using faith-sharing to propagate the institutional church, we would see faith-sharing as the end for which the institutional church is the means. The church is called to spread the gospel rather than propagandize for itself.

3. We would recognize that the gospel is constitutive of the church. The church has its being relative to the gospel. Therefore, the rock of our faith is not the institutional church; nor is it an apostolic authority such as Peter. The "rock" of our foundation is the new truth revealed in Christ.

4. We would also see that faith-sharing is not a "program" of the church. To the contrary, the church is a ministry of faith-sharing. If the gospel is normative, then faith-sharing does not take its shape, style, and content from the church. The church, to the contrary, must structure itself as a means of sharing the good news of Jesus Christ. If the gospel is constitutive of the church, then the church lives only as it communicates the gospel!

5. Faith-sharing is derived from our theology, not from our ecclesiology. We tend to do it the other way around. Our language gives us away. We talk about the church's evangelistic task, or the mission of the church, as if faith-sharing were the church's invention, the church's idea. But the derivation of faith-sharing is not an ecclesiological but a theological phenomenon. As we said, if faith-sharing has its roots in the living God, then the church, strictly speaking, does not have an evangelistic mission. The church is called to participate in God's mission for the sake of the world.

    Faith-sharing is not a program of the church. To the contrary, the church, when it is authentic, is a ministry of faith-sharing. You see, if faith-sharing is but a program of the church, the church is free to list it on newsprint as a priority this year and eliminate it next year. But God does not give us the luxury of debating whether faith-sharing is a priority, as if it were our idea. When we do this, our ecclesiology has taken charge of our theology. Faith-sharing is founded in God's love. It is God's idea and not the church's invention.

6. The fact that God's seeking, sending love reaches out to us through the history of patriarchs, prophets, and ultimately through Jesus Christ is ample proof that God ordinarily speaks to persons through persons.

7. Since faith-sharing is, in part, a response to our realization of what God is like, some understanding of the nature of God is necessary in order for conversion to happen. This, we take it, is the supreme importance of preaching and teaching in faith-sharing.

FAITH-SHARING FULFILLS THE GREAT COMMISSION

Not only is faith-sharing founded in God's love; it also fulfills the Great Commission (Matt. 28:19-20). It seems to us that this is the proper order, lest we allow the Great Commission to become a new form of legalism, a duty to God rather than a response to the grace of God. Now, we are not denying the fact that Christ commanded his followers to carry his message to all people and to the ends of the earth. Moreover, we would insist that we hear Christ's command: "As the Father sent me so I send you" (John 20:21, NEB). But we do not believe that command and commission are the primary forces behind our faith-sharing efforts.

Michael Green cautions us at this point by saying, "The obligation depends not upon the letter but upon the Spirit of Christ, not upon what he orders but upon what he is, and the Spirit of Christ is the Spirit of divine love and compassion and desire for souls astray from God."[10]

If we understand the scriptures, they seem to teach that law and commission grow out of grace. Again, look at the setting of the Ten Commandments. Prior to any divine imperative is a divine announcement: "I am the Lord your God who brought you out of Egypt, out of the land of slavery" (Exod. 20:1, NEB). The decalogue follows the exodus. Law grows out of the covenant.

Moreover, in the New Testament, priority is given to the gospel. The first word of Christianity is always *gospel*; moral exhortations and commissions follow. The Christ who called people to follow him in grace is the same Christ who turned around and taught people how to live with him responsibly and how to share faith effectively.

So law and gospel belong together. Both are needed, but the order of the two is crucial. The gospel comes first. The indicative precedes the imperative. Without the announcement of God's love, one does not have the motivation or the ability to obey commands and commissions. Commandment and commission grow out of the redeeming act.

We do not believe that our church members will be greatly motivated to share faith by simply heaping "oughts" upon them. ("You ought to do this or that!" or "You must be more committed and try harder!") We have been taking that approach for years and it has not worked very well. Grace, not guilt, motivates people to share faith. It is when the love of God becomes the great compulsion that faith-sharing becomes the Great Commission.

FAITH-SHARING FOCUSES ON TOTAL REDEMPTION

The redemption of society is another powerful motivation for those who advocate a whole gospel for the whole person in the whole world.

When we see the dire needs all around us, we are deeply moved. Our hearts ache because millions are forced to live unfulfilled lives, victims of poverty, hunger, oppression, and racism. We are deeply concerned when we see the threat of pollution and nuclear destruction hanging over the whole earth. It troubles us deeply to see people in bondage to inner compulsions such as gluttony, alcoholism, or drug dependency. It hurts to see some of our youth floundering in aimlessness. We are troubled by the decadence of our morally permissive society.

In Christ we see the answer to these and other deep personal and societal needs. Thus, we are moved to share the gospel by word and deed.

In the final analysis, the question of motivation cannot be answered theoretically or by some lofty argument. The question can only be answered by each person who claims to follow Christ. We would put the question this way: How much difference would it make in your life if at midnight you ceased to believe in Jesus Christ?

Some might find themselves having to reply, "Well, I suppose life would go on about as usual. I might have to surrender my ordination papers or I might have to resign my membership in the local church, but not necessarily so! I suppose I would get up in the morning, go to work, come home for dinner, watch TV until bedtime just as always. I would continue to play a round of golf once a week. I would certainly continue my work in the P.T.A. or Rotary Club. I would continue to vote a Democratic or Republican ticket, but I don't suppose it would make any other difference that I can think of."

However, those of us who have encountered the living God in Jesus Christ would have to say, "If at midnight I ceased to believe in Jesus Christ, I don't know how I could go on living. I have learned to say with Paul, 'For me to live is Christ.' Jesus Christ is the very center of my being. If I ceased to believe in him, all of the lights would go out of my sky, and I would be left in utter darkness. I think I would just want to lie down and die."

Now, we ask you this: If our faith matters that much to us, is there any person on the face of God's earth for whom it ought to matter less? If we could not live without Christ, can we lie down comfortably in our bed at night so long as there is one single person who has not heard the good news? Yes, the love of God constrains us to share our faith.

But what is the nature of the faith we share?

REFLECT AND ACT

1. What difference would it make in your life if you ceased to believe in Jesus Christ?

2. Imagine your own faith journey. Have you responded out of oughtness and fear, or have you responded to the gospel and God's love shared? Give specific examples.

3. As you move through today, tomorrow, this week, reflect on each day. When you have shared faith, when you have reached out, what has been your inner motivation? Is it a sense of oughtness, out of legalism and law, or are you compelled by love? Are there differences in your response to different situations? Reflect on specific situations.

4. On page 24 there is a thesis outlined related to the motivation for faith-sharing: (1) Faith-sharing is founded in God's love; (2) it fulfills the Great Commission; and (3) it focuses on total redemption. Read John 8:1-11. In what ways does this relate to the thesis?

5. When have you experienced *agape* love (making the giver and the receiver vulnerable) as a gift? When have you experienced love as that whose purpose was to possess? What was the difference for you as the receiver—or as the giver?

How do we move to sharing the vulnerability of God, as an act of the will? What difference does this make in how we love and respond and reach out?

3
The Nature of Christian Faith

The authors have spent many years engaged in the task of faith-sharing. By God's grace and with the leadership of the Holy Spirit, they have had the privilege of sharing faith in every section of the United States and in more than fifty countries around the world. We continue to do our best to multiply the witnesses for Christ by teaching others the basics of Christian faith and how to share their faith.

These experiences have left us with an indisputable conviction: The way we understand the nature of Christian faith has an enormous impact upon the way we go about sharing that faith. Therefore, if we are to share faith, we must first know the nature of that faith.

In this chapter we will keep our attention riveted upon the practical need to teach people how to share faith, while at the same time, we will not disregard the theological need to have all of our personal witnessing grounded in scriptures and consistent with the best that we know theologically.

DEFINING CHRISTIAN FAITH

Christian faith is a centered, personal, relational response involving trust and obedience.[1] First, Christian faith is *centered*. This means that Christian faith has a particular object. According to scriptures, the object of Christian faith is the living God revealed in one Jesus of Nazareth whom we call the Christ, Messiah, Son of the Living God. Immediately, we are faced with the particularity of Christian faith. Christian faith is not faith in general. To say that the object of Christian

faith is Jesus of Nazareth whom we call the Christ is to take the adjec-
tive "Christian" with all seriousness. We are not using the word *faith* in
any generic form.

Therefore, the object of Christian faith is not a philosophy of life
about which we may speculate, nor is it merely a system of ethical
ideals about which we may argue, nor is the object a set of doctrinal
propositions to which we must give mental assent. Again, the object of
Christian faith is the living God revealed in one Jesus of Nazareth,
whom we call the Christ.

Second, Christian faith is *personal* for two reasons. Faith is personal
because it is centered in a person; that is, its object is a living person.
Jesus is a living person because of the resurrection. Resurrection is not
merely an event that happened some two thousand years ago, which we
consider with amazement and awe. Resurrection is far more dynamic.
Resurrection means that Jesus Christ is alive right now!

In an International Seminar sponsored by the World Methodist
Evangelism Institute, one of the African delegates told the following
story. This man had the privilege of sharing faith with an African chief.
The chief said, "We believe in God already, but we want you to tell us
about Jesus Christ." Whereupon, the delegate told the story of the revelation of God in Jesus Christ. Beginning with the birth of Jesus, he did
his best to recount the story of Jesus' ministry.

When he told about the resurrection, the chief suddenly stopped him
and made the following observation: "I have known at least five people
in my lifetime who have come back from the dead." We are not accustomed to hearing such a thing in North America, but this would be
characteristic of what one might confront in the African culture. However, the African delegate was not at all daunted by this observation.
He responded, "Well, chief, tell me this, are these five people yet alive?"
The chief thought for a moment and said, "As a matter of fact, they are
all dead."

Our brother replied, "Sir, I have come to tell you of One who was
dead, is alive, and is alive forevermore." He is alive right now! And, we
agree with Paul—if we Christians do not believe that, then of all people,
we are most miserable (1 Cor. 15:14-20). Of its very nature, Christian
faith would have to be personal because its object is a living person.

Christian faith is also personal because it requires a personal
response from each human being. It is this demand for personal
response which respects the sacred right of rejection or acceptance on
the part of each human being. We can pray that another person might
have faith. We can do our best to create an environment in which faith
is taught and caught. But we cannot have faith for another person any

more than he or she can have faith for us. Faith is so decidedly personal, it demands that each must own that faith for himself or herself.

One of the authors and his wife have four children and four grandchildren.[2] Our grandchildren are perfect! Our children may not be perfect, but our grandchildren are perfect! In all humility we claim that we have endeavored to raise our children in a self-conscious Christian home. As infants our children were all taken to the altar and presented in Christian baptism. We did our best to teach them the meaning of that baptism so they could claim it for themselves. We always had daily prayer in our home. The children knew that Jesus Christ was the very center of our lives, and they realized the importance of the Bible in our daily lives.

Attendance at church has always been so much a part of our lives that we never stopped to think whether we should or should not go. However, in spite of the fact that we tried to maintain this Christian atmosphere in our home, and in spite of the fact that we earnestly endeavored to love all our children equally and treat them equally, nevertheless, we have known the meaning of rebelliousness.

This rebelliousness started quite early in the lives of two of our children. Not only did they rebel against Christian teaching; they tried to reject the values of a Christian home and establish values more akin to the peer group or subculture with which they identified. As parents we felt so helpless in this situation. We watched them make mistakes, and yet there seemed to be very little we could do besides love them, pray for them, and hold steady. Throughout this painful time of rebellion we learned the meaning of pain and vulnerability.

Had it been possible for us to have Christian faith *for* these children, we would have. But we could not. They had to own that faith for themselves, and eventually they did. During their time of rebellion, as parents we held steady and were available to them in times of need. Thus, faith is personal not only because its object is a living person but also because it requires a personal response from every human being.

Christian faith is also *relational*. It is relational first because it makes possible a right relationship with God. Scripture says, "For it is by his grace you are saved, through trusting him" (Eph. 2:8, NEB). Both the content and order of Paul's statement are important. Notice that grace is in first position. It is the grace of God which provides the basis for a relationship with God. Grace is the motivating dynamic in Christian conversion. Without the dynamic of prevenient and justifying grace, we could not repent or believe.

This divine grace of God is made operative in our lives by the power of the Holy Spirit. It is the Holy Spirit who opens our eyes to the liberating grace of God. The Holy Spirit breaks down barriers, builds bridges, and enables persons to respond. But it is through faith that this divine grace is claimed and appropriated. By way of faith we are brought into a right relationship with God.

Faith not only properly relates us to God; it also properly relates us to our neighbor. Here we confront the relational nature of Christian faith. One cannot be properly related to God and improperly related to the neighbor. The Christian's relationship with God is bound up in the relationship with the neighbor and the relationship with the neighbor is bound up with the relationship to God. We cannot claim to love God while we hate our brother or sister (1 John 3:14-16).

Christian faith also enables us to establish a right relationship with the self. Once properly related to God, the Christian is no longer victimized by a civil war raging inside. The peace treaty has been signed. "Therefore, now that we have been justified through faith, let us continue at peace" (Rom. 5:1, NEB).

Christian faith is so dynamic that it properly relates the human being with the whole ecological environment. It brings with it a new respect for and stewardship of God's creation. When we are properly related to God, our neighbor, and the self, we can no longer be content to treat God's creation selfishly and unthinkingly. The acquisitive appetite, which is born of unbridled greed and causes the human being to exploit God's creation, is overcome by a right relationship with God, our neighbor, and the self. This so fills our lives with respect for God's creation that the Christian refuses to rape God's good earth.

Next, Christian faith is a *response* of the total person. It is more than mere feelings. To base faith on feelings would be to plant one's feet upon shifting sand. Feelings are as fickle as the mist of morning. The foundation of faith is not what we feel or what we have done so much as it is what God feels toward us and what God has done on our behalf. Thus, the foundation of faith is not so much our commitment to God but God's commitment to us. Our commitment is a response to God's commitment. It is a response which involves body, mind, soul, spirit, sensibility, and will—the whole human being.

The biblical dynamics of Christian faith are summed up in two words: *trust* and *obedience*. Trust defines the relational and personal dimensions of faith. Trust is an excellent word for faith. Our very existence and identity are constituted by the pattern or network of trusts that we hold. There is a definite sense in which we are what we trust. We tend to treasure what we trust and trust what we treasure. Jesus knew this better than anyone and said, "For where your treasure is, there will your heart be also" (Luke 12:34, NEB).

The only appropriate response to the living God revealed in Jesus of Nazareth is ultimate trust. To trust God is to commit one's total self. To trust God is to rely on God and to allow one's self to be shaped on a deep level by the living God. Whether we are Christian, in the final analysis, does not depend upon where we live or where we hold our church membership but rather upon whom we trust.

Ultimate trust leads one to *obedience*. Response becomes responsibility. Here we are faced with the ethical dimension of faith. To trust God is to submit ourselves to the Lordship of Christ. This means that all of our lesser trusts and our previous trusts are called into question. If we truly trust God, we begin to realign the configuration of trusts that make us who we are. When God becomes our ultimate trust, we realign all other trusts accordingly. To realign our trusts is to realign life at its center. One favorite gospel song says it all: "Trust and obey, for there's no other way to be happy in Jesus than to trust and obey."

When Christian faith is understood as a centered, personal, and relational response involving trust and obedience, it has about it a contagion that is inevitable. It is so contagious and powerful that its spread is normal and natural rather than contrived. Once it is caught, it spreads from person to person.

If Christian faith is so dynamic and infectious, why are we seeing so little of this contagion within our movement? There are three powerful barriers to this dynamic understanding of Christian faith. These blockages are found in all of our congregations, and we need to find ways to identify and remove these blockages. These barriers are succeeding in undermining Christian faith by reducing it to something it was never intended to be.

BARRIERS TO CHRISTIAN FAITH

Barrier 1: Faith Is Believing Beliefs

Our people inadvertently fall into this understanding because of heavy use of the English words *belief* and *believe* to denote faith. In the English language the noun *faith* has no verbal form. We cannot say, for instance, *she faiths*. Therefore, we say, *she believes*. This is quite true both biblically and grammatically. However, at this point the plot thickens. Because *believe* is associated with *belief*, people assume that faith is *believing beliefs*. This creates great difficulty because the noun *belief* does not mean the same thing as *faith*.

Once people have reduced faith to belief, then the question arises, "What beliefs?" In the supermarket of competing denominations and non-Christian religions, we get a great many answers to this question. One group will say, "If you want to go to heaven, you must believe *these* things." Another group will say, "You must be kidding! If you really want to go to heaven, you must believe *these* things."

Still others will say, "Both of these groups are crazy! My Bible says if you really want to go to heaven, you must believe *these* things!" We know that one of the major barriers to sharing faith is that too many faith claims are foisted upon us. This blockage tends to reduce faith to belief and belief to a varying set of doctrinal propositions. Faith is robbed of its personal-relational nature, and people are bound to impersonal dogma. This blockage assumes that everything must be crystal clear, in black and white, or else faith is impossible.

This is an ideal system for those who wish to let someone else do their thinking for them. This attempt to reduce faith to merely believing beliefs has great appeal in our world, and this appeal is borne of our insecurity. In recent history people have had their values overturned. As the Lord said in *Green Pastures*, "Everything that is nailed down is a'comin' loose!" Moreover, many North Americans, as well as affluent people worldwide, whose primary source of security is found in what they own or possess, feel terribly threatened by anything that would tend to undermine that security.

Add to this the cosmic insecurity that comes as a result of the threat of nuclear holocaust, and you have a people who are very susceptible to security systems that will offer them simple, clearcut answers. They want neat systems that offer correct beliefs, and they wish to know that they are doing all of the correct things to merit salvation. Any questioning of the system is considered totally incompatible because propositional belief cannot tolerate any deviation from the stated dogma.

John Wesley called this propositional faith "a dead faith." He contended that it was dead not because it failed to believe but because its object was a set of opinions, notions, or propositions rather than the living God revealed in Jesus of Nazareth. In two illuminating passages Wesley spells this out. First he defines "a dead faith" as follows:

> *This faith is a persuasion that there is a God and a belief (of all the truths contained in His Word); so that it consisteth only in believing that the Word of God is true. And this is not properly called faith. But as he that readeth Caesar's Commentary, (though he believeth it) to be true, yet (he) is not properly said (to believe) in Caesar; even so he that believeth all the Bible (to be true) and yet liveth unGodly is not properly said (to believe in God).*[3]

Then Wesley points out the difference between "opinion" (what we prefer to call "proposition") and genuine Christian faith. Notice how he highlights the personal-relational nature of faith:

> *But what is faith? Not an opinion, no more than it is a form of words; not any number of opinions put together, be they ever so true. A string of opinions is no more Christian faith than a string of beads is Christian holiness. It is not an assent to any opinion or any number of opinions. A man may assent to three or three and 20 creeds; he may assent to all the Old and New Testaments (at least, as far as he understands them) and yet have no Christian faith at all . . . Christian faith . . . in its more particular notion . . . is a divine evidence or conviction wrought in my heart that God is reconciled to me through his Son, inseparably joined with a confidence in Him as a gracious, reconciled Father.*[4]

Finally, Wesley believed that this "dead faith," based upon propositions and dogmas, is simply not Christian faith. He says that Christian faith

> *is not a bare assent to this proposition, Jesus is the Christ; nor indeed to all the propositions contained in our creed, or in the Old and New Testaments. It is not merely an assent to any or all these credible things as credible. To say this, were to say (which who could hear?) that the devils were born of God; for they have this faith. They, tremblingly, believe, both Jesus is the Christ, and that all scripture, having been given by inspiration of God is true as God is true.*[5]

It is clear that John Wesley believed there must be a content to Christian faith, and Wesley, like Jude, would "contend for the faith that was once for all entrusted to the saints" (Jude 3, NRSV). Faith does have an object. However, he believed that content to be a personal act of trust and commitment to the living God revealed in Jesus Christ and not mere mental assent to a list of doctrinal propositions or opinions. Partly, Wesley's understanding of faith was due to his reaction against the Church of England of his day and its system of basing one's relationship to God on correct beliefs and moral rectitude. It was obvious to Wesley that a person could hold right beliefs and follow a strict moral life, and yet not be properly related to God, neighbor, self, and the world.

Like Paul, Wesley could see that Abraham's response to God was stereotypical of Christian faith. For Abraham, faithfulness meant walking by faith and taking risks. It meant leaving the security of the known and walking toward the insecurity of the unknown. It meant leaving the comfort of the familiar and walking off in the direction of the unfamiliar and the discomforting. It meant walking by faith and not by sight (Romans 4).

If we could take Wesley's dynamic interpretation of faith seriously and understand Christian faith as walking with God toward the unfamiliar and the unknown, we would not need to regard doubt and inquiry so anxiously. For, by definition, the opposite of faith is not doubt but distrust or mistrust. If we take Christian faith seriously, we need not be fearful of inquiry. After all, it is often the doubting side of the mind that enables us to discover deeper truth. The inquisitive side of the mind tends to play intellectual games with ideas, batting them back and forth until they are driven to exhaustion or to deeper truth.

Second, this dynamic understanding of the nature of Christian faith would help us see why the historic creeds never say, "I believe *that* God exists." Or, "I believe in the existence of God." As Wesley put it, "So does the devil." According to scriptures, the devils believe both that Jesus is the Christ, and that all scripture having been given by inspiration of God is true as God is true.

Here we confront one of the most important evangelism issues for those of us who live in North America. According to the polls, over ninety percent of all North Americans say, "Of course we believe that God exists." But, according to the polls, almost half of that percentage go on to say that this belief makes no difference in their lives. It is like saying, "Of course I have a neighbor named Ed Walton." But this only asserts our belief in the fact of Walton's existence. That is all.

The creeds take a different approach. They say, "I believe *in* God, the Father Almighty . . ." The small word *in* makes all the difference. If one says, "I believe *in* my neighbor, Ed Walton," this means one is involved in a relational act of trust, commitment, and allegiance. It means that a relational covenant exists between self and neighbor.

It is obvious that a huge group of those who tell the pollster George Gallup, Jr., that God exists use this "belief" as an inoculation against true Christian faith, that is, a vital, life-transforming, relational trust in the living God. They have good civil religion but no Christian faith. It is much easier that way. Almost any religion makes lighter demands than the call to a personal relationship with God. People will accept laws, ideas, systems of thought, or propositions much sooner than they will accept a personal relationship with the living God.

To say "I believe *in* God" means that I trust God; that I commit my allegiance to God; that I covenant with God. It means that I live out my life under God's righteous judgment, which has an impact upon my total existence.

If we take Christian faith as walking with God and taking risks, then churches will be affected. We educate in such a manner as to sometimes set our children and youth up for a fall. Sometimes we have treated education in such a way as to insinuate that our responsibility is to fill our children's heads with all the right beliefs and ideas.

One young woman, who grew up in a suburban church, attended two years of confirmation training. It was assumed that she was taught all the right things, and she was confirmed on Palm Sunday. Later she graduated from high school and went to the state university. During her freshman year she took a course in geology. Her professor was a Sunday school teacher in one of the nearby United Methodist churches, though she did not know this.

About midway through the course this woman confronted something in one of her readings that undermined one of the basic beliefs she had endorsed during her confirmation training. Once that belief was undermined, it was like a crack in the dike. All of the water in the reservoir began to rush toward that crack, and suddenly everything could be lost.

If we take seriously the Wesleyan understanding of the nature of faith, we need to highlight two important aspects in the educating of our children and youth.

First, we need to put tremendous emphasis upon the story line of the Bible. Some of our young men and women go to colleges, universities, and even theological seminaries, but they know neither the story of the gospel nor the stories of the Bible. We need to bathe our children and youth in the stories of the Bible.

Next, we need to put increasing emphasis upon personal experience. Wesley defined Christian faith as "a sure trust and confidence that Christ died for my sins, that he loved me and gave himself for *me*."[6] This personal experience of Jesus Christ is missing in our churches. Nothing can take its place. If this young woman had been given a dynamic personal experience of Christ, she could have approached her university education quite differently. She could have openly admitted that she did not have all the answers. However, though she did not know it all, she knew in whom she had believed and was persuaded that he was able to keep that which she had committed unto him against that day (2 Tim. 1:12).

Barrier 2: Faith Is the Opposite of Understanding

According to this view, if we have good evidence to prove something, we say we "know" it to be so. If we have only partial evidence, we say we "believe" it to be so. But, if we have no evidence at all, we tend to say we have "faith" it is so. This leaves the impression that faith is the opposite of understanding. Therefore, to be "saved by faith" sounds dangerously close to being saved by ignorance. We get the picture of someone who closes the eyes, breathes hard, and believes something in spite of all the evidence to the contrary. It is this misunderstanding which gives rise to much of the anti-intellectualism that plagues the Christian world.

Some of us will never forget an encounter with Dr. Harry Denman. He gathered us around the table in one of the board rooms at The Upper Room in Nashville. He read the passage concerning our responsibility–to love God with "heart, soul, mind, and strength" (Mark 12:30, NRSV). Then he turned to us and said, "I hope you young folks will never forget your responsibility to love God with your mind. It doesn't take a great mind to be a Christian, but it takes all of the mind that you have."

Harry Denman once made the following observations regarding Anselm. Anselm was one of the leading voices in the late patristic period, following the death of the first apostles. He asked, "Do you remember how Anselm defined theology?" Someone replied, "Yes, sir. Anselm defined Christian theology as faith seeking understanding." He said, "Do you know why Anselm defined theology that way?" "Well, because people are not saved by understanding; they are saved by faith." "Do you know why Anselm put it that way? Because faith must be in first position in order to have parity."

Someone asked, "What do you mean?" He said, "If people were saved by understanding, then a person with more intelligence would have a better chance at salvation. But, people are not saved by understanding; they are saved by faith. That's why even a little child can respond in faith. But once faith is in first position, we must spend the rest of our lives seeking to understand that faith. That's why a person never graduates from the School of Christ." He continued, "I hope you young folks graduate from Vanderbilt, but I hope you never graduate from the School of Christ. I hope you'll be lifelong learners."

We are grateful to God that we are a part of a tradition that highlights the need for both knowledge and vital piety. This creative balance is best expressed in a hymn written by Charles Wesley. In the hymn we are admonished, "Let us unite the pair so long disjoined, knowledge and vital piety." There is room for the tough mind as well as the tender heart. We are invited, through the Wesleyan tradition, to love God with the mind.

We praise God that we are a part of a tradition that does not treat faith as if it were the opposite of understanding but rather insists that Christian faith opens the door to greater and greater understanding. Faith, as Wesley interpreted it, opens the vestibule of knowledge. It is not restrictive or constrictive but liberating and freeing. It pushes back the horizons of our knowledge and invites us to explore the unknown.

One of the devastating side effects of the two blockages mentioned above is the way in which narrow propositional beliefs not only eliminate the excitement of inquiry but tend to constrict the mind. As one mountaineer put it, "People become so narrow-minded their ears scrape!" As the late Glenn "Tex" Evans used to say, "People become so narrow-minded they can look through a keyhole with both eyes simultaneously."

Barrier 3: Faith Is a Good Feeling

The tendency to reduce faith to little more than a good feeling is what we call the trend toward "faith in faith." It operates out of the popular notion that it does not matter what a person believes so long as that person believes so sincerely and fervently that it works. Faith is reduced to a psychological state or mood, and people are admonished to believe in faith. It is assumed that, if your faith produces a good religious experience, it is a true faith. Whatever you experience as good is good. And whatever makes you feel bad obviously must *be* bad. "Good is good and bad is bad. How do I know? Because my feelings tell me so."

For these people the real test of any faith is the religious experience accompanying it. They tend to preach that religious experience is the ultimate truth. Therefore truth is apprehended and evaluated by their infallible "feelings." They say, "If I feel good about myself, then things are right with myself." The outcome of the faith journey is understood in terms of finding self-identity, self-worth, self-respect, self-fulfillment, authentic selfhood, or feeling good about oneself.

God is a term often used to identify and describe the character of the religious experience that comes to those who quest rightly. Thus, *God* becomes a creature of our experience. The faith journey is our human journey to God, rather than God's journey to us or our journey with God. God's function and value lies in the use *God* can be to the quester. Faith is reduced to a psychological state, and people are admonished to believe in faith.

Paul Scherer characterizes this approach: "It adds up to something like this: Have faith in faith—it is of great therapeutic value. Get up every morning and stand erect in front of an open window, head thrown back, breathe deeply three times, every time with the words, 'I believe, I believe, I believe.'"[7] It doesn't matter what you believe so long as you believe it with enough intensity that it works for you.

When faith is reduced to a psychological state, then salvation comes as a result of one's success in cultivating or maintaining the proper state. Salvation is a reward given to those who attain the correct intensity of faith. People are, therefore, encouraged to believe "harder." Those who believe the best and the most are the ones who are saved the best and the most. Faith, then, becomes a "work," and people are thought to be able to justify themselves through the act of faith. The Bible, however, insists that the focus of faith is directed toward Someone outside the self: God, the gospel, and the Christ it announces.

The faith that is awakened by the gospel through the power of the Holy Spirit is not simply a psychological state which a person can maintain by trying hard or mastering a certain mental attitude, mood, or routine.

This barrier is so pervasive in our world that we must identify it as a powerful contemporary heresy. It often is expressed as little portions of Christianity combined with various teachings coming out of pop psychology, new-age ideology, and eastern religions. For many, feeling better about themselves appears to be more important than discovering faith in the living God. Yet the biblical tradition indicates that God is not intensely interested in our "feelings" but in our "doings." The text indicates that God acts on our behalf mainly to save us and to keep us going, and not necessarily to make us feel better. This would indicate that our feeling good about ourselves is no proof that we are right with God or that God feels good about us.

Thus, it is wrong to allow peak experiences to denote the very truth of things. In this narcissistic culture God would have us be more in touch with God than with our own feelings, our bodies, ourselves. God is certainly more reliable as a guide to truth. It might be more helpful for us to forget about our feelings and think only of God. Who knows, in so doing we might find ourselves feeling better in the very process.

If the object of Christian faith is the living God revealed in one Jesus of Nazareth whom we call the Christ, then to allow the self to supplant that object is a form of vile and selfish idolatry. Moreover, to assume that salvation comes as a result of one's success in cultivating and maintaining certain psychological states or moods is but another form of what Martin Luther called "works righteousness." This works righteousness may be dressed up in contemporary, sophisticated psychological language, but it is works righteousness, nonetheless, and severely damaging to Christian faith.

We are convinced that viewing faith as a centered, personal, and relational response of trust and obedience is not only a powerful biblical antidote to all three of these barriers, but it also provides the guidance we need in fashioning our understandings and strategies for faith-sharing.

If Christian faith is a centered, personal, relational response involving trust and obedience, what would it mean to share Christian faith?

REFLECT AND ACT

1. In their working definition of the nature of Christian faith, the authors say: Christian faith is a centered, personal, relational response involving trust and obedience.

   A. Christian faith is seen as personal in that we believe in the resurrection and the living Christ.

      • Remember resurrection stories in the New Testament. How did these affect the persons who experienced Christ's living presence?

      • How have you experienced the living Christ?

   B. Christian faith requires a response involving trust and obedience.

      • What does it mean in your life to trust God? In what specific ways does this affect the center and alignment of your day-to-day life and living?

      • What are the spiritual disciplines in your life which help you to center and focus your relationship to God?

      • In what specific ways does the Christian faith enable you to be in right relationship with your neighbor?

2. The authors believe that it is imperative to hear and pass on the stories of the faith.

   A. Each day this week choose one or two stories of the faith to reread. Take time to reflect on the life situations and how they relate to today. Take time to "hear" again the responses of trust and obedience and faithfulness.

   B. Find at least one other person with whom you will share stories of the faith this week.

3. Have you experienced, or are you experiencing, any of the barriers listed in the last part of the chapter? What was helpful to you in breaking through these blockages?

4
The Meaning of Faith-Sharing

Faith-sharing is evangelism. When attempting to teach evangelism in North America, Europe, and nations influenced by western culture, one confronts a great deal of negativism, stereotypes, and even hostility from a large percentage of the church membership. United Methodists and other Wesleyan churches often carry negative images of evangelism. Some people have been violated and exploited by a type of evangelism which has created nothing but guilt and resentment within them. Much of this negativism, however, is not justified. Many people use negative feelings and stereotypes to rationalize their lack of concern for and commitment to evangelism.

However, whether justified or not, these negative feelings exist and must be acknowledged by anyone who wishes to give leadership in evangelism ministries. Therefore, as a matter of strategy, we never feel compelled to use the word *evangelism* at the start. Rather, we have found it productive to help people confront their understanding of God and the nature of Christian faith. As we shall see, the way we understand God and Christian faith will have an impact upon the way we understand evangelizing and the way we go about doing it.

We recognize that people have radically different views regarding the nature of evangelism, and we know the necessity of starting where the people are. So it is helpful to address questions about the nature of evangelism from varying angles. During an East African regional seminar in Kenya, one of the authors had an opportunity to visit an animal park.[1] We got there by way of land rover and were not allowed to leave the vehicle. However, because it had a removable roof, we were able to take pictures from the top of the vehicle.

The first animal we saw was a giant bull giraffe. The African guide kept driving around and around this beautiful giraffe. Suddenly, one of the pastors in our group noticed a herd of elephants, and becoming very excited, tried to get the African guide to drive off in the direction of the elephants. The guide kept driving around the giraffe. Thinking that the guide had not understood his request, the North American pastor tried again to communicate that he wished to be driven in the direction of the elephants.

In perfect English the African guide said, "I know that you want to see the elephants, but you really haven't seen this giraffe. You see, here in Africa, we have animals so large that in order to truly see them you have to view them from many angles." Likewise, the issue of evangelizing is so large that you simply cannot understand it if you view it from a single angle. We will mention two.

METHODOLOGY

When people in our congregations are asked to define evangelism, they recite the method by which they themselves, or the largest number of people in their social network, came to faith.

For instance, if we were to ask Dabney Story, a member of a church in the hill country of northeast Mississippi, he would say, "Well, preacher, I'm surprised that you don't know that! Of course, evangelism is the annual revival." Dabney would say that with all the conviction he could muster. And the longer you listened to Dabney, the more you would get the impression that, as far as he is concerned, evangelism is revivalism. To hear him talk, you would think that the Holy Spirit is available to the church only during the third week of August. To be sure, many people come to faith in Christ through the annual revival meeting.

However, if we were to journey to Wisconsin and ask Marshal Owens the same question, he might say, "Why, of course, pastor, evangelism is our confirmation program." He would say this with the same depth of conviction that we heard from Dabney. The confirmation tradition is very strong in this region. Many of the local churches have one-, two-, and sometimes three-year confirmation programs. On Palm Sunday of every year busloads of children are driven down that confirmation route—some of them kicking and screaming!

Once confirmed, many of them, unfortunately, take their places in the ranks of what we call "CPE Christians." These are Christmas, Palm Sunday, and Easter Christians. They are regular attenders, but only on these particular occasions. When you talk with some youth and adults who have gone through confirmation training, some of them will speak as if confirmation Sunday were a type of "graduation exercise." Thus, some adults consider Christian education as something relevant only for children and youth. However, as we all know, many people come to faith in Jesus Christ through confirmation training.

If you were to ask our friend Sam to define evangelism, he would reply, "Unquestionably, the most effective evangelism is the Lay Witness Mission." (The Lay Witness Mission is a weekend renewal event which utilizes the testimonies of lay persons and the dynamics of group ministry.) Sam would proceed to tell you about the time when he entered the "middle-age crisis." It was as if his life were falling out at the bottom.

He looked at his relationship with his wife and had to admit that it no longer held the romance and excitement that he once knew. He looked at his children, now grown, and had to admit that they had not lived up to his expectations. He looked at his job and acknowledged that it was boring. There was a time when that job held tremendous excitement. But during his crisis, when the alarm sounded in the morning, he could scarcely muster enough energy to get his feet over the side of the bed.

Although surrounded by people, Sam admitted to himself that he was desperately lonely. As a member of a United Methodist church for over twenty years, he had made and paid his pledge and attended only four or five times per year, but it seemed quite meaningless.

One morning he was so miserable that he decided to return to church. Much to his amazement, the entire service had been taken over by lay people. Suddenly, he found himself listening to the testimony of a person who, like himself, had reached the middle-age crisis. As he sat there, he found himself saying, "For heaven's sake, that man is talking about me!" Today he cannot fully describe what happened, but suddenly he found himself kneeling at the front of the church and there he discovered a relationship with God and a vital faith that he had never known. Many people in our congregations have discovered vital faith through the ministry of the Lay Witness Mission.

Our friend Esther would say, "Evangelism is none of the above. As far as I am concerned, evangelism is presenting these four biblical and spiritual laws." Esther might give the impression that the church must load its guns with a volley of four gospel shots, aim those guns at the people, and get people to pray the "sinner's prayer." Depending upon a person's theological perspective, those people are saved whether they realize it or not. Many people come to faith as a result of this method.

Others would say that "evangelism is the small-group movement." These persons insist that revelation never happens monologically. You must get people together knee-to-knee and eyeball-to-eyeball. They say, "If you have truth to convey, you must never spoil it by preaching it. In preaching, people are like chickens on a roost and about that alert!"

Again, many people discover faith in Christ in the dynamic atmosphere of small, accepting *koinonia* groups. These groups allow for the free expression of fears and faith, doubts and devotion. In that dialogical dynamic the living God breaks through. Many of you discovered faith in Christ through such a small-group experience.

Others would insist that real evangelism can be found only by listening to one of the popular North American television evangelists. Some of these converts insist that mainline churches have become apostate churches. It is no longer necessary or productive to belong. They insist that you can believe without belonging. If you know the Lord in your heart, if you are on an evangelist's mailing list, and if you are a loyal American, God will prosper you in all things. You will become healthy, wealthy, and wise. Many people are discovering faith in Christ through television ministries, and they testify to a new life of meaning and fulfillment.

To be candid, there are ways by which and through which people come to faith in Christ that are an affront to us. It seems that despite bungling methodology and the poorest sort of theology, the grace of God does break through, people respond, and their lives are transformed. After years of struggle, we have come to a conclusion that has helped us unravel some of the ambiguities related to the methodology of evangelism. The conclusion can be stated in one simple sentence: **No one way is <u>the</u> way, but each way, by God's grace, can become <u>a</u> way.**

This brief statement has helped us in two significant ways.

First, this statement accents the powerful grace of God. People may employ the worst, most bungling methodology, but God's grace is greater and people's lives are transformed. This does not excuse poor methodology, but it does insist that the grace of God is greater.

Second, this statement enables us to be truly ecumenical. Our nationwide and worldwide ministries have challenged us to discover what Thomas C. Oden envisions: honest ecumenism.[2] Thereby, we have overcome the bureaucratic and elitist ecumenism which continues to hold some people in oppressive bondage. As a result, we can affirm God's grace working in the lives of persons even though the theology and methodology leave much to be desired.

There are, however, at least two subtle dangers involved in viewing evangelism solely from the angle of methodology. The most obvious danger is the temptation to take one method, describe it as God's only way, and then impose that particular method upon every human being.

This can become an insensitive form of religious tyranny. Not only does it fail to respect the freedom of the Holy Spirit to work in countless ways, but it also refuses to acknowledge the enormous variety that resides in the human family and the tender and sensitive way in which God deals with each person.

A man, while working in the forest, suddenly fell into an abandoned well. He tried to climb the slippery sides of the well but to no avail. Finally, in complete desperation, he sat down in the muck and mire at the bottom of the well and began to pray, "Oh God, please send someone to rescue me from this well." Suddenly, he heard a voice from above. He looked up and there silhouetted against the sky was the face of a man. He cried out to the man above, "Please save me from this well."

The man above heard his plaintive cry and threw a rope down the well with the instruction to fasten the rope about his waist. With the aid of the rescuer above, the man was able to climb the slippery sides of that well, and he was saved! It was such an exhilarating experience of "being saved" that the saved man spent the rest of his life chasing after people and throwing them down wells! Remember, methods are necessary as means but demonic as ends; and all methods are under the judgment of the gospel.

Evangelism defined as method is also dangerous because it mutes part of the primary witness of the church. For example, some preachers tend to overplay Paul's experience on the road to Damascus. The pattern or method of Paul's conversion is held so constantly before the people they assume Paul's experience must be typical of all conversions. When these same people look at their own Christian pilgrimage, they find very little that is remotely similar to what happened to Paul on the road to Damascus.

They have not been persecutors of the church. They have not been stricken blind. They have not heard God calling out their name in English. If Paul's experience is typical, and if they find so little in their own experience that correlates, then they might assume that they are not Christians and therefore have no story to tell.

Most of the people in North American United Methodist churches have had experiences more similar to the Emmaus Road than the Damascus Road. On the Emmaus Road, two brothers are walking together and are suddenly joined by a mysterious Stranger. They know that the Stranger is present, but they cannot name the Stranger. Nevertheless, the Stranger is invited into their house, and together they share food. In table fellowship, in an atmosphere of hospitality, in the breaking of bread, the scales suddenly fall from their eyes, and they are finally capable of recognizing the risen Lord. In retrospect they say to one another, "Were not our hearts burning within us while he was talking to us on the road?" (Luke 24:32, NRSV).

We are convinced that the Emmaus paradigm contains much that is akin to the actual spiritual pilgrimage of great numbers of people. We encourage them to tell *their* story. It may not be Paul's story; it may not be our stories; but if it is their story, then why mute this powerful witness?

Some pilgrimages illustrate the Damascus Road, while others are typical of the Emmaus Road paradigm. To stereotype a certain model, order, or process as the "only way" constitutes a serious perversion of the biblical perspective, and it puts a tragic limitation on the scope of the gospel's power.

EUANGELION—PRESENTATION OF THE GOSPEL

Fortunately, there is a more productive angle of vision than that of method. In an earlier chapter we pointed out that evangelization has its origin, pattern, and basis in the nature of our missionary God and in the activity of the first evangelist, Jesus Christ. One of the common themes which underlies the heterogeneous collection of materials in the Bible is its missionary focus. Despite the diversity between the various parts of scripture, the Bible is, nevertheless, the story of God's redemptive purpose and activity in history.

The primary word for evangelism in the New Testament is the Greek noun *euangelion*. It is a compound of two words meaning "good message." We have shortened that to "good news" or "gospel." It is impossible to conceive of evangelizing without the gospel. The Greek verb *euangelizomai* means "bringing, spreading, or announcing the *euangelion*, the good news or gospel." So, evangelizing describes the spreading of the good news of the gospel.

The words *euangelion* and *euangelizomai* were common words when the New Testament was written in the first century. They meant to bring good news about a great event such as the announcement of a new age to come. These were precisely the meanings picked up by the followers of Jesus to describe the great event of Jesus' coming into the world. As a result, the books telling the story of Jesus became known in the second century as "gospels," while their authors were known as "evangelists."

Let us be clear that the constituent element in evangelization is the good news of the kingdom of God. Therefore, evangelization is never present unless the good news of the kingdom of God is present. Fundamentally, evangelization is an ongoing process of communication involving this gospel.

This definition is quite different from the popularized understanding of evangelism. For several years one of the authors worked on an experiment in a classroom setting.[3] He would point to a specific person and ask the class, "What am I talking about if I say to you, 'I have just evangelized Joe Smith'?" Invariably, the class would respond, "It means you have converted or saved him."

This is a common mistake. We forget that it is God who converts. We are responsible to evangelize, and that which we evangelize or spread is the gospel of the kingdom. Joe Smith will be worse off if *we* save him or convert him! When people become *our* converts, they tend to become *our* clones! We must never forget that the people who followed Jim Jones into Guyana were *his* converts.

Leander Keck and John R. W. Stott insist[4] that "in the New Testament 'to evangelize' does not mean to make converts as we sometimes use the word." It is the spread of the good news of the gospel, regardless of results, which constitutes evangelizing. Thus, Stott says, "Evangelizing is neither to convert people, nor to win them, nor to bring them to Christ, though this is indeed the first goal of evangelizing."

Unfortunately, in our success-oriented culture, we tend to confuse the process of evangelizing the gospel of the kingdom with the goal of that process, which is conversion. Therefore, many of the definitions of evangelizing are actually definitions of conversion, and this serves only to confuse. Our desire is that conversion will happen, but to be biblically accurate, we must insist that the essence or core of evangelizing lies in the faithful presentation of the gospel of the kingdom by word, deed, and sign.

If we could hear this biblical word, it would be liberating. It would teach us that we need not fret or worry over the results of evangelizing. Rather, we ought to fret over whether we have made known the gospel of the kingdom. We are convinced that many of our people shy away from evangelizing not only because they do not know what it is but because they are afraid of failure. The only failure we ought to fear is that of failing to spread the gospel of the kingdom. The results are in God's hands.

Emphasizing that the essence or core of evangelizing lies in the faithful presentation of the gospel does not mean that people are free simply to dispense the gospel with no thought given to either the arena or field for faith-sharing or intelligent analyses regarding results. Obviously, abundant harvests depend upon faithful and thoughtful seed-sowing.

Seeds sown on the surface of an interstate highway will not render the same results as seeds sown in receptive, cultivated, and fertilized fields.

However, no matter how thorough our demographic studies, no matter how fervent our prayers, no matter how sensitive we are to cultural realities, no matter how thoughtful and indigenous our models for evangelism, the results are still in God's hands and we had better know it. The apostolic church understood this reality. Luke clearly states ". . . the Lord added to their number daily those who were being saved" (Acts 2:47, NIV).

Therefore, it is important to put the proper object to the verb. There is a tendency to define evangelization in terms of the recipient or the target of the message, or else we define it in terms of the result (that is, whether or not people are converted), or we define it in terms of the methods that are used. We forget that the object of the verb *euangeli-zomai* in the gospels is the good news of Jesus or the good news of the kingdom or the Word of God.

We do not evangelize people or nations or even structures. We evangelize the gospel. **Evangelizing is not something we do <u>to</u> people but something we do <u>with</u> the gospel.** Obviously, we do not go around announcing or spreading people. If people hear the gospel and, under the inspiration of the Holy Spirit, trust the good news of Jesus, they convert; that is, they repent or turn around. They switch kingdoms.

We insist that the proclamation of the gospel of the kingdom of God always includes an invitation to recognize and to accept in a personal decision the personal saving Lordship of Jesus Christ. But, this Lordship also means that we renounce the kingdom of sin and accept responsibilities in terms of God's love for the neighbor. When we let Christ into our hearts, he brings the neighbor with him.

This repentance, conversion, or *metanoia* results in a transformation of our attitudes and styles of life. It is a dynamic process involving turning from that which holds us in oppressive bondage and turning to that which liberates us to new life. It always demands reconciliation with God and with the neighbor. It means leaving our old sources of security behind, our old "trusts," and risking the walk of faith. It makes possible a personal encounter with the living Christ, but it also contains a call to repentance and obedience which is addressed to nations, groups, and families. It is a call to switch from war to peace, from injustice to justice, from racism to solidarity, from hatred to love.

Thus the message of the gospel of the kingdom of God is broad enough to include the individual conscience of every human being as well as the collective conscience of groups and nations.

EVANGELIZATION DEFINED

Evangelization is the process of spreading the gospel of the kingdom of God by **word, deed, and sign** in various contexts, through the power of the Holy Spirit, and then waiting and watching in respectful humility and working with expectant hope.[5] This definition informs us that the three primary means of spreading the good news of Christ are word, deed, and sign.

Writing to the church in Rome, Paul gave an excellent summary of the primary means. He wrote, "For I will not venture to speak of anything except what Christ has accomplished through me to win obedience from the Gentiles, by word and deed, by the power of signs and wonders, by the power of the Spirit of God, so that from Jerusalem and as far around as Illyricum I have fully proclaimed the good news of Christ" (Rom. 15:18-19, NRSV).

WORD AND DEED

The gospel must be made both visible and verbal. To employ one means without the other is to truncate the gospel. In the biblical literature, word and deed are held together in an unbroken rhythm. In creation God spoke and creation happened. In the evangelization of Jesus there is no polarization between proclamation and action, or salvation and history. In Jesus, word and deed do not fall apart. Jesus has integrity. His words ring true to his lifestyle and his life supports his words. Each illumines the other. Thus, by word and deed Jesus brings the claim and the power of the righteous reign of God (the kingdom of God) to bear on the whole of humankind.

We discover this same wholeness of word and deed in the evangelization of the early church. In the Acts of the Apostles, proclamation and good works are inextricably tied. There is a fusion of preaching and serving. Most often proclamation is done in the midst of ministries to the physically afflicted, in the midst of the healing of hurts, in the midst of hostile inquisition, and in the midst of head-on collisions with the oppressive processes of the world.[6]

The biblical rhythm demands that the verbalization of the gospel must take place in the midst of doing it. The ministry of *kerygma* (proclamation) must run concurrently with ministries of healing, serving, nurturing, liberating, reforming, and empowering. Announcement of the Kingdom must be both verbal and visible, and one never asks which is more important. That would be like asking which is more important, breathing in or breathing out. It depends upon which one was done last! Obviously, proclamation and lifestyle must buttress one another.

During his work in the Central Appalachian Highlands, one of the authors spent one month working with the Red Bird Missionary Conference.[7] He had the opportunity to spend three days with the thirteen missionary pastors who were working devotedly with the people of the Central Appalachian Highlands. One day in an extended dialogue, one of the missionary pastors observed: "You cannot assume that the people who live in the hollows associate Jesus Christ with the work of Red Bird Mission."

The author was stunned by that remark and repeated it to make certain that he had heard correctly. A number of haunting observations were made. Everyone agreed that The United Methodist Church shows tremendous proficiency and commitment when it comes to doing the deed of the gospel. We do the compassionate deed from the best of motives, and we do that deed with skill and commitment. However, we are reluctant to name the Name in whom we do the deed.

This failure to "name the Name" leaves an ideological vacuum in the minds and hearts of the people. As a result, other sect-type churches and cults come right along behind us, and they fill the ideological vacuum left by our silence. Through our good deeds of compassion we can dispel the devils of ignorance, hunger, and oppression. But if we do not name the Name, the house is often left empty. Therefore, seven other devils come and take up occupancy there, and the latter state of the person is worse than the former (see Luke 11:24-26).

Let us not forget that we are called to offer a cup of cold water in the name of Jesus. If we only name the Name, we are dismissed as irrelevant, but if we only give the cup of cold water, we are quenching the physical thirst but leaving spiritual thirst unsatisfied.

The first edition of this book was published in 1986. Since that time the authors have experienced a growing conviction that the time is right for the church to put primary emphasis upon verbal witnessing to the gospel of Jesus Christ. The strength of this conviction culminated in the publication of *Let the Redeemed of the Lord SAY SO!* (Abingdon Press, 1991).

We felt compelled to write this book because in recent history we have moved through a period in which some church leaders have tended to emphasize doing the deeds of the gospel almost at the expense of verbal witnessing. The vindication of our conviction can be seen in the fact that the English version of *Let the Redeemed of the Lord SAY SO!* has been printed in four countries and the text has been translated and published in six languages. But why is there such a reluctance to speak up and speak out?

We believe that our reluctance comes as a result of our fear of vulnerability. At what point are we most vulnerable as Christians—when we do a good deed to help some brother or sister or when we raise to speech the most profound convictions of our lives and put those out before the people? We are far more vulnerable when we state forthrightly the profoundest convictions of our lives.

Sometimes it is far easier to settle with simply doing a good deed for a poor person, but this is not sufficient. People not only hunger for bread for their stomachs; they also hunger for the Bread of Life. This Bread cannot be purchased at anyone's bakery. It comes through a right relationship with the living God in response to the gospel of the kingdom of God.

SIGN

Sign is an important means of gospel communication, although it must be acknowledged that like every good thing in this world, sign can be trivialized and misused and thus made to look illegitimate. There is no truth, idea, or means that has not been abused by someone, and we freely admit that this means of gospel communication (signs and wonders) has suffered greatly at the hands of selfish and unscrupulous people. However, no matter how abused, this is never an excuse for abandonment of that which is clearly part of the biblical record.

In the Bible, signs and wonders often serve to validate both the message and the messenger. This can be seen in the Old Testament. God's presence and power were indicated through such means, especially at the time of the exodus and during the journey in the wilderness. This was also true of the ministry of Jesus (Acts 2:22) and the apostles (Acts 5:12). Paul certified the same in his letter to the church at Corinth (2 Cor. 12:12).

Signs are visible tokens of invisible realities that are spiritually significant.[8] During an evangelism seminar in Ghana, West Africa, one of the authors[9] had an experience that confirmed this statement. After presenting a definition of evangelizing which did not contain "signs" as an important means of gospel communication, he was challenged by one of the West African bishops, who said, "Where is the rest of it? Why did you exclude 'signs and wonders'?"

The author proceeded to list his reasons and confess his neglect. The bishop responded, "That's a pity! For you do not understand!" He then instructed the author to print the word *significance* on the chalkboard. Next he said, "Now underline the word *sign* in significance." Once the author had done this, the bishop said, "Whatever gives significance to Christ is a 'sign'."

He then proceeded to teach us that "sign" is inclusive of more than miracle healings, though these are also significant. He pointed out other signs such as great art, stained glass windows, sculptures, dance, poetry, and especially the Eucharistic signs of bread and cup.

Since that time, the authors have added an exciting dimension to their gospel communication. Now, they not only look at all the forms of art differently, but by the power of the Holy Spirit, they have witnessed miraculous manifestations of the Holy Sprit in their faith-sharing. Like Paul, they can now attest to the communicative power of "signs and wonders."

In a world evangelism seminar in South Africa, leaders from seven countries sought a clear vision and strategy for evangelizing the gospel in the region. After more than three days, it became obvious to all that a key strategy for sharing the gospel was through the ministry of healing. In a continent which has experienced so much violence and pain, that which is desperately needed is the healing of the land and the people. This **sign of healing** is needed to fully convey the wholeness of the gospel among a people who have experienced brokenness and suffering. Authentic faith-sharing includes word, deed, and sign.

Moreover, we are more convinced than ever that most perversions come when the communicator attempts an exclusive emphasis on one of these basic means of communication at the expense of the others. In addition, we have observed that faithful faith-sharers and healthy congregations are precisely those who have discovered a fundamental balance in word, deed, and sign.

WAIT AND WORK

The final phrase in our definition of evangelization has to do with what we call the posture of the faith-sharer. Faith-sharers must wait in respectful humility. This means faith-sharers are constantly driven to their knees. We are utterly powerless without the power of God to quicken the seed of the Word of God, and bring forth new life. We are totally dependent on the power of the Holy Spirit. Only the Spirit can draw people to the kingdom. One might sow and another water, but only God gives the increase.

Luke insists the power for witnessing comes *after* the Holy Spirit baptizes the church. Without the vivifying power of the Spirit, we are powerless. The Spirit is the breath of the body. Without the Holy Spirit the church is breathless and powerless. There is no alternative to this sequence.

But not only are faith-sharers driven to their knees in respectful humility; they are constantly being raised to their tiptoes in expectant hope. Hope is evoked in the Christian as a result of response to the good news of the gospel of the kingdom. The message that God's deliverance has dawned in the new age of Jesus of Nazareth, in his victory of life over death, love over hate, reconciliation over alienation, evokes hope in the church. The church lives in the conviction that the risen Christ is available to everyone and at every geographical point. The risen Christ is present in his world. Being filled with the Holy Spirit, the church goes forth to spread this gospel of the kingdom and to develop congregations all over the world.

When the eschatological (future vision and hope) incentive of this dynamic gospel of the kingdom ceases to be our major reason for faith-sharing, we are looking at a bleak future. When the Tennessee Valley Authority announced a series of dams on the Tennessee River, a small but historical community discovered that it would be buried beneath the water. Its future was closed; therefore, the people no longer painted their houses, mended their fences, or preserved their fields. The closed future immobilized the whole community.

It is the widespread loss of hope and confidence in the truth, power, and relevance of this gospel of the kingdom which, more than anything else, impedes faith-sharing. For not only is the gospel of the kingdom the saving power of God; it is also that which energizes the church with expectancy. Without the message of the gospel of the kingdom, life cannot be lived in joy, expectancy, and hope. Without the note of joy, expectancy, and hope, the church gives an uncertain sound, and its members do not gird themselves for battle. They become quite content with the four walls of their church. Therefore, one of the most incessant tasks of our day is to kindle the true hope of the gospel of the kingdom of God.

There is a rhythm in word, deed, and sign, but there is also a rhythm in working and waiting. We are driven to our knees in utter dependency upon God and simultaneously raised to our tiptoes in expectancy, knowing that the Word of God will not return to God void. It will accomplish that for which God sent it. We know that some seed will fall upon good soil and bring forth a seven-fold harvest.

THEOLOGICAL GUIDELINES FOR FAITH-SHARING

From our discussion of the nature of God, the nature of faith, and the nature of faith-sharing, what have we learned that will guide us in our faith-sharing? Here we outline five implications that serve as guiding ideas, which will be developed in forthcoming chapters:

1. Sharing Christian faith does not mean that we are trying to persuade others to adopt a point of view, but rather we are pointing persons to a Person, Jesus Christ.

2. We are called to introduce people not to a plan, or proposition, or an airtight argument. Rather, we are called to introduce people to a Person and his kingdom.

3. Jesus Christ does not call people to a religion. Rather, Jesus Christ calls people to himself and to the kingdom of God. There is much confusion over this guideline.

    One of the best illustrations of the difference between religion and faith can be seen in Exodus 31 and 32. In these chapters, God called Moses to Mt. Sinai, where Moses received the two tablets of stone written by the finger of God. Here you find the first axiom in understanding faith. Faith always requires the initiative of God. God acts first, and we respond in terms of God's action. Moses had ears to hear. He trusted God and obeyed God and went to the mountain to receive the tablets of stone. Faith teaches us that God is always seeking those people who have been made in God's own image.

    However, while Moses was on the mountain, the people decided to do a very religious thing. In religion, people seek God, but they ordinarily seek a god which suits them. They want a god who will lay few, if any, demands upon them and allow them to live as they please. The gold rings were stripped from the ears of the wives and daughters, melted down, cast into a mold, and made into the image of a golden calf. The people prostrated themselves before the god they had created and danced in frenzy around the golden calf. This teaches us that people will make enormous sacrifices for religion and religion will make fools out of people.

Jesus does not call us to religion but to faith. This point must be made again and again in a world which insists that religion is a good thing and that it does not matter what religion one holds as long as one holds it sincerely. Both of these ideas are based on the assumption that religion is inherently good. However, the Bible never says that religion is inherently good. To the contrary, the Bible insists that religion can be exceedingly evil. The prophets of Baal were very religious, but they were evil to the core. Those people who gave Jesus more trouble than anyone else were the religious people of his day. They dogged at his heels constantly, trying to discredit his ministry and get rid of him. Jesus Christ does not call us to religion. Jesus Christ calls us to himself and to the kingdom of God.

4. People give their lives to God, not because God sends them a tract or an advertisement but because God sends Jesus Christ. Here we discover that our faith-sharing methodology is founded on how God did it, and our attention is focused on the Incarnation. Incarnation insists that God does not bombard people with slogans and bumper stickers. In the person of Jesus Christ, God comes to the people and God walks the roads with people. Therefore, if we do Christian faith-sharing we will not be out trying to hustle for God or merchandise Jesus. To the contrary, we will find ourselves entering into the woundedness of people, even as Jesus did.

5. Our study of the nature of God, the nature of faith, and the nature of faith-sharing leads us to the conclusion that our best witness is always undergirded by our deepest relationship. We must explore the evangelistic potential in honest-with-God human relationships, but first with respect to our definition of faith-sharing we must describe the settings or contexts for presenting the good news.

REFLECT AND ACT

1. How would you respond if someone asked you, "What is evangelism?" How do you think people around you would respond?

2. One way of looking at evangelism is through methodology (confirmation, revival, Lay Witness Mission, etc.). In your own experience, what methodology or methodologies have been helpful? Through what other means has grace been experienced by others around you?

3. Has your Christian experience been more like Paul's on the Damascus Road or more like the Emmaus Road? In what specific ways is this true?

4. Biblical images of word and deed:

Scripture	What was the word?	What was the deed?
Acts 8:26-40		
Acts 3:1-10		

   Reflect for each day this past week: How have you spread the gospel by word and deed? Are you more prone to word or deed? If it is one or the other, what might be some barriers that prevent you from doing both together? What will you do to be more intentional in spreading the gospel by both word and deed?

5. What are signs? What role can signs play in faith-sharing? How does God use signs and wonders to equip us for faith-sharing?

6. Reflect on your experiences of faith-sharing in this past week. What specifically has brought you to prayer? In what specific ways have you experienced your dependency upon the Holy Spirit?

5
The Arena for Faith-Sharing

Our failure to share faith is occasionally not only failure to understand the nature of God and the nature of Christian faith but a
failure to communicate with people. An urgent question for the
faith-sharer in our day is how to build a bridge between the language
of the church and the language of the modern world without copying
the world and compromising the gospel. We can easily fall into the trap
of pandering to people's wants rather than ministering to their needs.
We can yield to the temptation to find out what people want and give it
to them, but this results in a failure to share the fullness of the good
news of the kingdom.

On the other hand, there is the temptation to dictate the terms of the
gospel, and the situation of the hearer is completely ignored.

The Christian faith has been neither accepted nor rejected by the vast
majority of people. For many, it has simply not come as a genuine
option in their lives. Often the failure to leap this gulf is not so much a
theological shortcoming but a malfunction in the process of communication. We must discover the points of contact between the Christian
message and the needs of the hearers.

A pastor shared a delightful story of a teenager in the church choir
who said that he would like to carry his pocket radio with him to
church and listen to the worship service which was being broadcast live
on radio. The pastor replied that it would be fine with him. In the congregation sat the young boy on Sunday with the radio plug in his ear,
listening to the worship service. During the sermon the pastor noticed
the boy was patting his foot, and the pastor knew the boy had switched
stations. The Word was being proclaimed, but it was not heard because

the hearer was on a different frequency.

Eugene Nida, a communication specialist and Bible translator, describes a model of the communication process: Source, Message, and Receiver.[1] He further states that communication does not take place in a vacuum but in the context of culture, a person's world. It is the culture which ascribes meaning to the various symbols used in communication. In our culture we make an "A-OK" sign with our hand, but in another culture the same sign is an obscene gesture. This variety of meanings in relation to culture shows up especially in terms of idiomatic sayings.

In a group of people who were joking with one another, a woman said to a man from Korea, "You are pulling my leg." The man replied in astonishment, "I have not touched your leg!" It is the culture which ascribes meaning to words and deeds.

THE DIAGNOSTIC IMPERATIVE

Unless we understand the receiver's language and world, we shall fail to communicate the good news of the gospel. A missionary to a beautiful island in the South Pacific was killed because he did not know the culture. For the people on this island, the hair on a person's head is special and must not be touched. The missionary did not know this, and in his greeting, accidentally brushed the hair of the chief. Having violated a very important cultural taboo, the missionary was killed. The consequences of our failures may not be so drastic, but sometimes in our faith-sharing we fail to communicate because we do not know the people and their world.

Jesus focused upon people and their needs. The New Testament reflects this perspective. Jesus saw the man who was sick. He discovered Zacchaeus in the tree. Jesus looked upon the woman. He noticed the children who had come to see him. Here is illustrated the necessity to see, hear, and understand the needs of people. This is the diagnostic imperative in faith-sharing.

It is interesting to note the implications of this imperative in the parables of the sower (Mark 4:3-8) and the seeds growing secretly (Mark 4:26-29). The parable of the sower does not put a great deal of emphasis upon the methods of the sower or the high quality of the seed. The emphasis falls upon the preparation and the receptivity of the soil. This is seen in highlighting the condition of the soil, the impact upon germination, the growth, and the fruit. The message of the parable is two-fold: You don't sow until the ground is plowed and assurance is given that some seeds will certainly germinate!

The parable of the seed growing secretly doesn't put the emphasis upon brilliant human methodology but rather upon such things as the *discernment of the farmer* and the *timing of the harvest*. First, the farmer knows what God is doing and will do if the seed is scattered on the ground. Second, when the crop is ripe, the farmer acts by applying the sickle. This fits well with our earlier observation affirming faith-sharing as God's idea. It also highlights the necessity of human cooperation in the process of gospel communication.

The harvester is sensitive to the prevenient grace of God preparing human lives to the receptivity of the gospel, and the harvester is willing to take appropriate action at the right time.

This parable teaches us about the process of faith-sharing:

1. We need to know much more than we often do about the people we seek to reach with the gospel. Who are they? Why do they live as they live and do what they do? What is really important to them? What determines their lifestyle?

2. We need to help them discover those points in life which are so deep they require more than a natural explanation if they are to have a full meaning.

3. We need to ask and look for those points of contact where the gospel is likely to be relevant and meaningful.

4. We need to recognize that the prevenient grace of God works in all persons to prepare for the sowing of the gospel. This may be expressed in different ways in different people. It may not be expressed as "I need God" but may be communicated in other ways, such as "Is this all there is to life?" "I want my life to count. Is there purpose to my life?"

BEGINNING WHERE PEOPLE ARE

Faith-sharing involves beginning where people are. We hear Donald Soper say, "We must begin where people are, rather than where we would like them to be."[2] The point of contact is between the good news of Christ and a person's specific need, desire, or motive. We are certain the gospel speaks to human needs and aspirations. Therefore, we listen for the questions which are raised. We must not only know that Christ is the answer; we must know the questions people ask.

This principle is not new. It is seen in the early church and the missionary movement. Latourette's *History of the Expansion of Christianity* tells how the early church, despite many obstacles, made great inroads into the Roman Empire. The early Christians were able to correlate the message of the gospel to several dominant needs of the people of the Roman Empire.[3]

One of the needs was loneliness. Many had been uprooted from home and clan. To engage people in their loneliness, the early church offered the *koinonia* of the community of believers. The open, accepting, loving fellowship of the early church was in itself a dramatic message. People acknowledged that they could see how the early Christians loved one another.

Another dominant need was a quest for truth. There were many religions, philosophies, and cults which were an expression of this hunger. To this need the early church spoke the *kerygma*, the message of Jesus Christ, whom the early church believed to be God incarnate and the ultimate revelation of truth.

The first-century Roman world had a need for God. People worshiped unknown gods (Acts 17) with the hope that they could be rightly related to some form of ultimate meaning. It was an incredible word of good news to hear that God had acted in Jesus Christ to "put us right" (Romans 5).

Many people who were looking for a higher moral standard of living in a decadent society were attracted to the ethical teachings of Christianity. In addition, the message of the Christians was that one could be empowered by the indwelling Christ to live a new life. The Christian faith is unique in that it not only insists upon the ethical imperative but offers the power to fulfill such a demand.

The fifth great need was reflected in the widespread desire for immortality. The religions of the day were not convincing and did not offer much hope for life beyond death. The early Christians preached the central message of the resurrection of Jesus Christ. When the early Christians proclaimed that nothing, not even death, could separate believers from the love of God, people responded to the invitation to believe. It is Latourette's contention that Christianity prevailed in the Roman world because it engaged more clearly and explicitly the people's needs than did other competing religions.

By beginning where the people are, we must proceed with caution. George Hunter points out that there are important ethical principles in appealing to human motives.[4] For example, a Christian realizes that many people know for sure what they want, but they may not know what they need. This means the faith-sharer looks beyond the conscious "wants" to see the underlying needs. In addition, the Christian may not share the faith to fulfill just any desire that people might have. There are human needs which are basic to human life—love, meaning in life, belief in eternal life—to which the gospel can be offered as fulfillment. But there are some desires—greed for money or passion for control over people—which are rooted in a broken relationship with God. The Christian faith is shared, not to fulfill these wants but to convert these desires.

With the awareness of this ethical dimension, we must ask the question: Where are the people? Who are the people around us, and what are their basic needs? We are called to understand and feel human need if we hope to share the Christian faith. We now review how others have expressed this assessment and understanding.

ASSESSING HUMAN NEEDS

Canon Bryan Green in *The Practice of Evangelism* perceived that human beings are motivated creatures. He insisted that the faith-sharer be in touch with and engage the following summary of needs: It may be the fear of death or of something else; it may be a deep sense of loneliness; it may be a weakness of the will, wanting to do right but failure to achieve it; it may be a sense of moral failure, with accompanying guilt and shame; it may be particular sins that are on the mind; it may be a lack of purpose in life, the aimlessness of living; it may be the very evil of the world, with a general sense of frustration and intellectual despair in the face of it.[5]

Another person who communicates on a regular basis with people who are outside the church is Donald Soper of England. He contends that people today express their needs very differently than they did two or three generations ago. The secularization process in the Western world has affected persons in significant ways. One is the shift from a "basic knowledge to fundamental ignorance about Christian matters."[6] Once people celebrated "holy days," but now it is "holidays." Even the courts in the United States have decided that Christmas is not necessarily religious, and a creche can be displayed in public places.

Today one cannot assume that persons have any knowledge of the Christian story. George Gallup, Jr., discovered in 1982 that less than half of the USA public can name all four Gospels.[7] Many people today live out their lives, go about their business, and make decisions without any knowledge of the living God.

Soper contends secondly that people today are far more life-conscious than death-conscious.[8] A century ago people lived with an acute consciousness of the reality of death. However, today people, especially in the Western world, expect to live much longer. Instead of struggling with mere survival, many people ask: Is there meaning in life? People want to live, really live, and many try to cram all they can into life.

A third modern shift in consciousness is from guilt to doubt.[9] This does not mean that persons are free from anxiety, but the anxiety is not based on an awareness of being separated from God. It is a more fundamental doubt about the reality of a God who knows and cares for them. People say they believe in God, but doubt that this belief makes any difference in their lives. People are anxious and feel at risk. As a result, people turn to quick fixes in their lives. They basically doubt that life can be better.

A fourth shift in persons is away from a profound sense of the need for God to a curiosity about Christianity.[10] We recall that even in the late fifties, in working with an "outsider," often the person would indicate an awareness of need for God, or a need for the church. But today that has shifted. Today, persons often state, "I have everything. Tell me why I need what you have to offer." They do not perceive that they need what they think the church has to offer. This is a crisis of perception and understanding. However, persons may be curious about Christianity or the Christian lifestyle, just as they are curious about the latest guru from the East.

A fifth major shift in people is from a sense of belonging to one of isolation and alienation. As the world has become an increasingly urban society, this has resulted in persons being alienated from nature, power, and neighbors.[11] If one lives in a controlled urban environment, one can ignore the cycle of nature. If one is separated from the land, one is cut off from power, particularly political power. If one lives in a huge metropolis, one's understanding of neighbor is different.

As a youngster growing up in the Southern Appalachian Mountains, one of the authors lived in a community where his father was born. In fact, he lived across the creek from the house where his father was born, which was a few yards up the creek from where his grandfather was born! In such an environment, it is easy to know one's neighbor. Today, however, the authors live in cities in which they do not know all the people on their street. There is a loss of community.[12] These changes in contemporary society are important for a faith-sharer to perceive.

In a book by Paul E. Little, we find another assessment of human need. He discusses seven basic human needs which are helpful contacts in faith-sharing. They are: (1) inner emptiness, (2) purposelessness, (3) fear of death, (4) desire for inner peace, (5) loneliness, (6) lack of self-control, and (7) desire to integrate thinking.[13]

It is interesting to note Reuel Howe's assessment of human need.[14] He says that these needs are often expressed in profound questions. "Who am I?" and "Who are you?" raise the basic question of identity. Every time a person moves into a new set of relationships, these questions are asked again. Other profound questions which people verbalize are, "How can I really become all that I was meant to be? How can I know that the fundamental purpose of my life is fulfilled? What shall I do with my life? Is there love?" These are basic questions. They point up people's longing for a sense of identity and purpose. This longing often leads people to give themselves in shallow commitments to a great variety of cultural, social, and economic gods.

In a real sense, people are never irreligious—they are other-religious. People today continue to worship idols that let them down. Therefore, they move from one idol to another. In faith-sharing, it is important to be alert to people who are moving from idol to idol. Often they are open to the good news of Christ if we can catch them between idols!

In a conversation with one of the authors, the noted theologian Albert Outler pointed to a similar view of basic human needs. He says that we desire the following:

- Identity—the need to know who we are.
- Liberty—the need to be free.
- Productivity—the need to feel and know that life counts for something.
- Serenity—the need to be content with a sense of fulfillment in life.

There is no universal consensus on what human needs are. Moreover, what speaks to one person does not speak to another. Therefore, in the same act of communication we reach some while missing others. Keith Miller shares the following:

> *One time after I had spoken to an adult class which I had been teaching for some months, a man came up and said, "Good lesson! I think that was the first time I really heard the Gospel," and he actually seemed to mean what he said. But a few seconds later someone else in the same group commented (with at least equal sincerity), "Well, you've taught some good ones, but that one really missed. It just didn't sound like the Gospel! Besides, people aren't interested in the problem you talked about anymore."*[15]

We feel, as do others, that the "Hierarchy of Human Motives" as developed by Abraham Maslow can offer some help at this point.[16] It provides a perspective for structuring human motives, and a framework for understanding human behavior. Maslow's hierarchy of human need is as follows:

> 7. Aesthetic needs
> 6. Desire to know and understand
> -
> 5. Need for self-actualization
> 4. Esteem needs
>   (A) self-esteem
>   (B) esteem from others
> 3. Love and belonging needs
> 2. Safety needs
> 1. Physiological needs

Maslow's theory says that these needs are basic to human personality, but they are not all in evidence at the same time. These needs, according to Maslow, are fulfilled in a sequential ascending hierarchy. Until the physiological needs, such as sleep, food, and water are met, they are dominant. Once these physiological needs are met, the safety needs move to the front of a person's desire. The safety needs are seen in the desire to be stable, secure, and free of danger. To know that one is free of harm and that the future is secure is an important motive appealed to by the advertising world. When the security need is dominant, the hierarchy looks like the following:

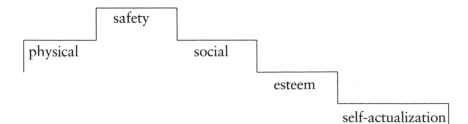

But when the physiological and security needs are "satisfied," the need to belong and to be loved moves to the dominant position. It is diagrammed like this:

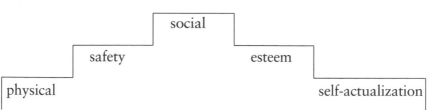

The need to be loved is basic in human nature. It is seen in many stages of life. For example, it is center stage in most youth who crave acceptance by their peers. Until this need is fulfilled, persons will go to extensive efforts to satisfy it. Once this social need to belong is satisfied, then, the esteem needs of a person become the most important. A person desires to be respected and appreciated by others. A lot of human behavior can be understood in light of the desire to be recognized and affirmed by others because of accomplishment and achievement in work and society. Without this need we would not have many plaques of appreciation being displayed in churches, offices, or homes. Each person has this need for esteem.

When the "esteem" need is met, then "self-actualization" becomes the need which motivates human behavior. This is the desire to be all one can be. Here is the drive to maximize one's own potential. People want their lives to count, to fulfill their basic purpose in life.

Maslow lists two needs that are not placed specifically on the hierarchy since they sometimes fit in any of the three highest areas. The desire to know and the appreciation of beauty cut across the three higher needs of belonging, esteem, and self-actualization. This is illustrated on the earlier chart by a broken line. (See page 70.)

This structure of human motivation helps to discover points of contact between the good news of Jesus Christ and the felt needs of people. We must recognize that the hierarchy is not neatly packaged in people. The way people express these basic needs will vary. It is not likely that someone will say, "How can you help me with my esteem needs?" More likely, we will hear or observe the needs expressed in different ways. Without question, if a person is hungry, we begin with physical bread. Jesus said that people cannot live by bread alone, but he did not say that people live *without bread.*

The Maslow structure can alert us to the different needs of persons. When someone says, "I feel that I am wasting my life," we are alerted to the need of self-actualization. However, when someone says, "I am just not appreciated, or no one seems to notice what I do at work," then we know that the esteem needs of that persons desire satisfaction. When someone shares, "I always feel I am on the outside looking in," we know this person deeply needs to belong and to be loved and accepted.

Now, in this assessment, we are not simply desiring to understand human need as an end in itself but as a means to enable us to love others as God loves them and appropriately share the good news of Jesus Christ.

ESTABLISHING CONTACT

We observe four key principles in establishing points of contact for sharing faith:

1. Enter into the Other Person's World

The Incarnation is not only the message of our witness; it is the model for our faith-sharing. God enters our world, and we see the glory of God. We are called to empathize with people. This is more than simply feeling sorry for people. To empathize means that we attempt to feel and see the world from the other person's perspective. We try to imagine what it would be like to be in the other person's shoes.

Jesus met people at their point of need. To a woman who was thirsty, he offered living water. To one racked by guilt, he offered forgiveness. To another, who needed to do a beautiful deed, he offered world-wide recognition. To another, who was alienated from family and neighbor because of his business activity, he offered a visit in his home and salvation to his whole house. To a woman suffering from a terminal illness, he offered wholeness through her faith. To one who was accustomed to controlling his own destiny by his religious activity, Jesus offered new life in the kingdom of God by being "born again."

Jesus entered the world of the other person and used it as an opportunity for offering good news. He challenged Simon Peter at the height of his strength. "Come with me," he said, "and I will make you fishers of people" (Matt. 4:19, NEB). This was offered, not because Simon's boat had sunk; he was a reputable businessman. Jesus did not ask him to become weak but offered him a greater challenge than any he had known. Jesus appealed not to Simon Peter's weakness but to his strength.

By entering the other person's world, we discover their needs and share faith in relation to their needs. If a person needs a sense of security, the providence and faithfulness of God is good news. If the need is to belong, the *koinonia* of the church offers a great resource for faith-sharing. The desire to be loved is addressed by the amazing grace which declares that God loves us first. Our fundamental needs for esteem are met by grace. The availability of God's grace for all people means that we are all-important, significant, and of great value. People who want their lives to count are challenged by the mission of God in the world. All are invited to participate in the creative mission to establish the kingdom of God.

The multi-level dimension of human need is addressed by the multi-faceted good news of the gospel of Jesus Christ. Most often we share a combination of the facets of the gospel in order to appeal to the multiple needs of people. The encouraging word is that there are sufficient resources in the gospel to meet all human needs.

2. Speak in the Language of the Hearer

This is the miracle of Pentecost. Luke writes, "Each one heard . . . his own language spoken" (Acts 2:6, NEB). This means that the one who shares faith seeks to use a language which is familiar to the hearer. It is easy to assume that because we know the meaning of a word everyone knows that same word and same meaning.

The brother of one of the authors is the head of a university engineering department.[17] During a visit he eagerly introduced the author to members of the faculty and explained their research projects. Finally, in desperation the author pointed out that his language and ideas may be familiar to an engineering professor, but not to a pastor.

In faith-sharing we are inclined to use words which are familiar to us, but these words may not be recognizable to the other. It is for this reason that persons who are in the same network or social circle can communicate so effectively—one athlete to another, one teacher to another, one banker to another, one farmer to another, one friend to another, one youth to another, one physician to another, one carpenter to another, one lawyer to another, and one neighbor to another.

If we live in a culture in which more than half of the people cannot name the four Gospels, we can assume that many do not know the meaning of much of the language that we use inside the church. Therefore, we are called to translate, interpret, and define the language of faith in terms of the hearer's perspective and context.

3. Be Sensitive to the Passages in People's Lives

Most often these passages increase the level of receptivity to the gospel. People are not always receptive. Part of the urgency in faith-sharing is to be alert and sensitive to those times when people are open to Christian faith. McGavran and others, such as Win Arn and George Hunter, see this as a most important factor in evangelizing.[18] Jesus talked about the appropriate time of harvest. We are called upon to become aware of the times when people are responsive to the good news.

People who are inquiring about faith are receptive. People who visit a church indicate receptivity. As people move through various passages in life, they may be receptive. Win Arn points out many important passages in people's lives:[19]

Death of a spouse	Trouble with in-laws
Divorce	Outstanding achievement
Marital separation	Spouse starts work
Jail term	Starting or finishing school
Death of a close family member	Change in living conditions
Personal injury or illness	Revision of personal habits
Marriage	Trouble with loss
Fired from work	Change in work hours
Marital reconciliation	Change in residence
Retirement	Change in school
Change in a family member's health	Change in recreational habits
Pregnancy	Change in social activities
Sex difficulties	Mortgage or loan under $10,000
Addition to family	Easter season
Business readjustment	Change in sleeping habits
Change in financial status	Vacation
Death of a close friend	Christmas season
Mortgage or loan	Minor violation of law
Son or daughter leaving home	Change in work responsibilities

While working with those who are receptive, we dare not neglect those who may be resistant. In many Christian conversions, it is the cumulative impact of many witnesses which results in repentance and faith. You may be the one present at the time of a person's acceptance of God's grace in Christ, or you may be number ten on a list of twenty faith-sharers before that person is responsive to the gospel.

4. Recognize that the Holy Spirit Prepares People to Be Responsive to the Presentation of the Gospel

This highlights Wesley's teaching on *prevenient grace*. Wesley uses this term to speak of God's initiative, God's going before or "prevenience." As we stated earlier, prevenient grace is rooted in the nature of God, and it primarily manifests itself in the action of God in Jesus Christ. Accordingly, Wesley contended that grace is "prior initiative," which makes "every human action, a reaction; hence, it is preventing grace." John Wesley insisted that "salvation begins with what is usually termed . . . preventing grace."[20]

Therefore, it is important to note that God takes the initiative in salvation. Thus, the process of salvation begins not with the human problem but with divine initiative. It is God's prevenient grace that evokes an awareness of human need leading to repentance and faith.

Faith-sharing begins with the living God who seeks long before our seeking begins. The Holy Spirit prepares persons to respond. We are called to be faithful sharers of the good news of God's grace in the arena where people live and die. This divine call confronts us with important questions regarding our identity and vocation.

REFLECT AND ACT

1. Look at the four shifts in secularization in the Western world as outlined by Soper:

   A. Do you celebrate holidays or holy days? What can you do to make your own celebrations truly holy days? How can you use this in faith-sharing?

   B. Where do you find sense to life? What is the most important thing in life for you? Where do you think people around you find meaning in life?

   C. How does trust in God make a difference in your life? How do you share this?

      This week be conscious of ways you can share faith by sharing the difference that trust in God makes in your daily living.

      How does trust in God make a difference in the lives of persons around you?

      What difference could trust in God make for others?

   D. If persons feel they have everything, what would you tell them God or the church has to offer in their lives?

2. Think of two persons in your circle of acquaintances who are not actively related to the church.

   A. What do you perceive as their idols?

   B. Do you know persons who are in the process of shifting from one idol to another? How might you share faith with them?

3. In the next two days listen to the conversations of persons around you.

   A. What needs do you hear them expressing? (See pages 67-72.)

   B. How does God's story, the good news of Jesus Christ, relate to their feelings?

      In relationships this week, empathize with persons, get inside their stories, try to feel with them to understand their life situation. What is the good news that relates to their situations? Begin to share faith with at least one person by sharing the good news specifically related to their life story.

The Identity and Vocation of the Faith-Sharer

We have considered the fundamental prerequisites for faith-sharing. We have seen how faith-sharing is founded in the very nature of God. We have understood the nature of Christian faith and what it means to share that faith. We have described the challenges to communication presented by our modern world and how the gospel meets the specific needs of people. We must ask: Who is responsible for faith-sharing? What are the identity and vocation of the faith-sharer?

Although the authors are ordinarily referred to as ministers, nevertheless, they are a part of the laity. Further, although most readers are referred to as laity, nevertheless they are responsible for ministry. At face value this sounds very confusing, but scripture will support our position.

In the New Testament there are many important words that depict Christian responsibility, and some of these words are crucial to our understanding of faith-sharing. The first is the Greek word *laos*, which means laity or people. Another is the Greek word *kleros*, which ordinarily means clergy. Who are the laity and what is the relation of the laity to the clergy? It seems that in God's divine planning the identity of the one is bound to the identity of the other, and this is fundamentally at the root of many problems in the church.

WHO ARE THE CLERGY AND LAITY?

When both the laity and the clergy are meeting together in a place of worship, there are basic differences and similarities. The clergy are those persons called by God out of the laity and invested by the church with authority to perform certain functions in the life of the gathered community. Clergy are "called by God to a lifetime of specialized ministries among the people of God" (From *The Book of Discipline of The United Methodist Church—2000.* Copyright © 2000 by The United Methodist Publishing House; ¶ 137, p. 93. Used by permission). This is the reason for putting emphasis upon "call" and "ordination."

Once those who are called fulfill basic requirements outlined by the denomination, the church invests them with fundamental authorities. Elders, called to a ministry of Service, Word, Sacrament, and Order, are given authority to preach the Word of God, to administer the sacraments, and to order the life of the congregation (*The Book of Discipline, 2000,* ¶ 323, p. 209). Deacons, called to a ministry of Word and Service, are given authority to proclaim the Word of God and to lead the people of God to connect the worship of the congregation with service to the world. In worship, deacons assist elders in the administration of the sacraments. In the world, deacons assist laity as they discover and claim their own ministries of service in the world (*The Book of Discipline, 2000,* ¶¶ 319–320, pp. 200–201).

The authority given is in the form of an investiture. It can therefore be taken away if the clergyperson is proven unworthy of such an investiture.

Then who are the laity? According to scripture, the laity are the people of God, a royal priesthood, a holy nation, claimed by God and given the mandate to proclaim the triumphs of the One who has called them out of darkness to light (paraphrase of 1 Peter 2:5, 9-10). Thus the laity are the church—a community of people who owe their existence, their solidarity, and their corporate distinctness from other communities to one thing only: the call of God.

Notice that the laity are called. Clergy are not the only called ones. This can be seen in Ephesians 4: "I entreat you, then—I, a prisoner for the Lord's sake: As God has called you, live up to your calling" (v. 1, NEB). This clearly indicates that all of the Christians in the church at Ephesus were both called and responsible to live up to their high calling. Moreover, the writer of Ephesians indicates that each Christian at Ephesus has been given gifts for ministry. He declares, "But each of us has been given his gift, his due portion of Christ's bounty" (Eph. 4:7, NEB). "All Christians are called through their baptism to this ministry of servanthood in the world to the glory of God and for human fulfillment" (From *The Book of Discipline of The United Methodist Church—2000.* Copyright © 2000 by The United Methodist Publishing House; ¶ 125, p. 89. Used by permission).

According to First Peter, the laity are both a "priestly people" and a "missionary people." As a part of Christ's royal priesthood, each Christian is responsible to be a priest to the other. In addition, each is claimed by God to proclaim the triumphs of the very God who called all of us out of darkness to marvelous light.

First Corinthians 1:9 and Romans 1:6 teach us that God has called us all into the fellowship of God's Son. God has called us to belong to Jesus Christ. Here we see that God's calling is directed to the whole people (the *laos*). This means every member of the body of Christ without any distinction or partiality. Ephesians 2:13-16 teaches that Christ has abolished all barriers of race, nationality, class, and sex. This is the abolishment of all privilege and status. The church is one people undifferentiated.

It is against this call of God that the real scandal of "clericalism" may be seen. "Clericalism" or "clergyism" attempts to concentrate status and privilege in the hands of the clergy, which obscures the essential oneness of the people of God. According to scripture, there is no difference in status and privilege. The fundamental difference is in functions and the invested authority to fulfill those functions. In spite of this fact, ever since Constantine thought he did the church a favor by becoming a Christian, there has been a tendency to manipulate a difference between authority and function into a difference in status and privilege. This creates an immense gap between the laity and the clergy.

God's intent is that the church should be a worshiping and witnessing community in which both of these functions belong to the whole people. The clergy cannot monopolize them and the laity cannot escape them. The ministry of Christ was given to the whole congregation. It is the clergy's function within that context not to be the center of the show but to find a way of embodying a serving ministry for the whole people of God. The model role for the clergy is one of servanthood.

However, over the years the church has come to distinguish sharply between clergy and laity, between religious and secular vocations. We find no scriptural grounds for these distinctions. Certainly there was no division into clergy and laity among Jesus and his little band of followers. In manner, speech, and mood Jesus identified himself as what today would be called a lay person; the disciples, who from our vantage point, were like lay persons and were actually the ones sent out to preach, teach, and heal. In the New Testament, there is little sign of the deep vocational difference which eventually infected the church. This disease still takes its toll.

Many people continue to believe in what we call the "sacred hierarchy." That is, God is at the top, beneath God are the bishops, then the clergy, and at the bottom is the lowly lay person. Have you not heard people say, "I am *just* a lay person." Have you ever made that remark?

Let's unpack the word *just*. Lay persons actually use this word to mean "only," "merely," "simply," or "lowly." Then they will turn to phrases such as, "without authority," "not as good as," "ill-prepared or equipped," "lacking in skills" or "not ordained." Finally, someone will mention "not responsible"! The progression always moves in that direction. Many lay persons have shared that they sometimes feel like "Santa's little helpers." That is, they feel that their responsibility is to help the pastor fulfill that pastor's ministry. But according to the Bible the effectiveness of the clergy's ministry is dependent upon whether the laity seize *their* ministry.

Again, we wish to emphasize, the New Testament word for clergy (*kleros*) refers not to those who occupy a special place among Christians, and the word for laity (*laos*) refers not to a passive-recipient part of a congregation but to *all* Christians. All are called to ministry, and all are ordained by God for service.

Unfortunately, the word *laos* contained the seeds of its own decay. Originally, the Greek word meant "people," that is, any people or crowd of people. In the secular Greek language, the word referred to the population of a Greek city-state. In the Bible, however, *laos* was first used in reference to the people of God—meaning Israel. It was sometimes used to contrast the Jews or the first Israel with the Gentiles (Acts 4:10).

However, in the New Testament understanding of the new Israel, the word was used to include all God's people inclusive of Christian Gentiles. It was, then, an inclusive word, meaning all the members of a people. Thus, we can see it was natural to use this word to denote the masses of Christians. However, the word was also used to distinguish the masses from their leaders. The *laos* of a Greek city-state were thus distinguished from the *kleros*, who were their magistrates.

In the course of time the English word became even further debased until, in current vernacular, the word *lay* often is synonymous with an amateur, a nonprofessional, or the unqualified masses. Because of this the word has taken upon itself an apologetic, condescending nuance. Thus, when a person says, "I am just a lay person," the organization of the Greek city-state has won out over the New Testament. But, in the New Testament the two words denote the same people.

In the biblical tradition, ordained persons were never thought of as ontologically distinct from other members of the congregation. It is true that ordained persons have a special function or share in Christ's ministry. But the difference is in ordained persons exercising their charges of word, sacrament, and order. Other members of the *laos* were not primarily distinct in essence, nature, or reality but in function.

WHO IS RESPONSIBLE FOR MINISTRY?

When the laity and clergy are meeting together in a place of worship, there are fundamental differences and similarities. However, when the laity and the clergy leave the place of worship and go into the world, not only is there no difference in status and special privilege; there is no difference at all. The one word that brings the two words *laos* and *kleros* together is the word *ministry*.

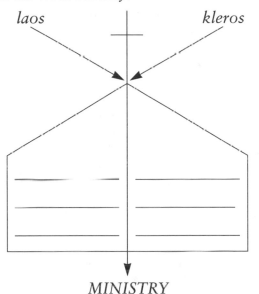

In the New Testament the word *ministry* is never used to denote the responsibility of one select, fully ordained group. The word *ministry* is always used to denote or designate the responsibility of the whole people of God. The clergy are those called of God to serve the laity, that is, to teach them and train them for their life, their work, and especially for their witness and ministry. The ministry of Christ was given to the congregation (Eph. 4:11-13). The ordained ministry is responsible for particular functions at a particular time in the life of the church. These are functions of the gathered community. When the church is gathered, the task of the ordained person relates to the function of word, sacrament, and order. But when the church scatters into the community and the world, there is no real difference in function, responsibility, or accountability for ministry.

We must overcome the heresy which teaches that the task of ministry belongs only to the professional worker in the church. Nothing is more crippling to the work of Christ. The idea that we hire a minister in order to do our ministry for us is totally incompatible with what scripture teaches. However, in local churches across the world people have developed the idea that somebody else will share the faith. Many laity have convinced themselves that they are not adequate: "We are not trained like others. We are not sure we will have the right words to say. We do not know the scriptures, and we do not know all of the doctrines of the church."

Most church members think of the church as a religious institution to which they belong rather than a dynamic fellowship of disciples living in immediate communion with their Master with his mission as their primary concern. Sadly, many church members tend to think of the church as existing for their sake, and it would be terribly disconcerting for them to learn that it is the other way around. Remember William Temple's famous statement: "The church is the only institution in the world that exists for the sake of non-members."

Nothing has been more deadly to faith-sharing than the idea that it is a special ministry done by select people who can perform in unusual ways, and only at special events and seasons of the year. The responsibility for faith-sharing belongs to the whole people of God. The Spirit came to the whole people of God, giving power to bear witness to Jesus Christ. Never did the early church think or act with the notion that the ministry of spreading the story of Jesus belonged only to those specially selected apostles.

In Acts (8:1-4, NEB) we read of a terribly violent persecution against the church in Jerusalem. "And all except the apostles were scattered over the country districts of Judea and Samaria." Now notice the clear message of this story as the scriptures continue, "As for those who had been scattered, they went through the country preaching the Word." Who were these scattered ones? Everyone except the Apostles went all over the country districts proclaiming, preaching, announcing, and spreading the good news of the gospel.

What a difference it makes to know that every one of us has been called to the joyful responsibility of sharing faith. This means that lay people do not exist as helpers of the clergy, but all of the people have this task of witnessing to the good news. It means, too, that no pastor should ever feel alone in ministry since all the people of God are in this ministry together. Just the difference in the sheer numbers of witnesses would have a powerful impact in spreading this good news of Jesus Christ.

This understanding of the *laos*, the people of God, as the ministers in the work of sharing faith helps us respond to the work of the church rather than being captured by "church work." We are all called to this full-time responsibility of sharing faith. No one is called to part-time Christian service.

WORD BECOMES FLESH

The scriptures teach that the Word becomes flesh in people (John 1). The Word is the Word, but in order for the Word to be communicated, it becomes flesh. A century ago Phillips Brooks maintained that truth comes through personality. Truth and personality are not synonymous. Personality is the vehicle for conveying truth. Our task is to spread the news of God's story in the light of our own particular stories with the hope that persons will respond in faith. In the early church, the people experienced the reality of the presence of the living Christ and they had to find a way to share that reality. In like manner, when God's story (the gospel) intersects my story, I must share that story with others.

It is through the lives of real people that we see and hear the story of God's redeeming grace. There was a little girl who had a brief line in a Sunday school program. All she had to say was "I am the light of the world." She rehearsed it. She practiced it again and again with her mother. She learned it very well.

The program came and the little girl was confident, but the mother was nervous. When the little girl saw all the people, she forgot her line. She twisted and turned. Her eyes looked at the ceiling. Her mother tried to prompt her. Carefully and slowly the mother's lips formed the words, "I am the light of the world." The little girl straightened and with a deep breath and loud voice announced, "My mother is the light of the world." It is through people that gospel communication takes place. The very Word of God is shared from person to person and people to people. In a real sense we are the hands, feet, and tongue of the living Christ.

One of the most important elements in faith-sharing is the person who shares faith. *Who* says it has much to do with the response to what is being said. Eugene Nida points out that the psychological factors are very significant in the communication process.[1] The reaction of the other person is dependent upon that person's attitude toward the source. An interesting experiment was conducted with students. A statement equivalent to "revolution is a good thing" was distributed to a group of students. Some of the students had the author of the statement as Jefferson. However, on the other papers Lenin was cited as the source of the statement. The reaction of the students was dependent upon their attitude toward the presumed source.

Therefore, who we are as communicators has a profound influence upon the quality of the communication and the receptivity of the other. This is not new. Aristotle spoke of the *ethos* of the speaker. The *ethos* constitutes the being and character of the communicator. Aristotle claimed that the *ethos* was the most important element in the process of communication. This means that a Christian witness is understood as the testimony given, but it is also understood as the one who gives the testimony. Witness refers to both the message and the messenger.

We have all heard the admonition that we must practice what we preach. This is true, but it is equally true that we preach what we practice. We cannot separate the witness from the witnesses. The distinctive lifestyle of the Christian is the very fiber out of which comes the word of faith. It is a tragedy when our lifestyle blurs the effectiveness of our witness. As we said earlier, our words and deeds belong together. Each illumines the other. We share faith in word and deed. God is calling us to this holistic understanding of faith-sharing.

In one country where Christians were not allowed to share faith openly, a youth told the story of how he witnessed. On Sunday morning he walked to church. He took the biggest Bible he owned and put it under his arm as he headed toward church, but he did not go the shortest way! He took the long way. He wound through the streets with the Book. It was his way of inviting people to church. We do witness by our deeds and practices as well as our words.

YOUR STORY MATTERS

Each Christian is unique and each Christian's story is unique. Each Christian should tell that story at the appropriate time. Many contemporary Christians have pulled back at the thought of verbally sharing faith with another. Witnessing or talking about Jesus Christ is difficult. Many people find that it is like drawing their breath in pain to talk about Jesus Christ. Most find it much easier to work around the church building than to go and talk with people in their homes about Jesus Christ. Talking about serious matters is a difficult thing. Husbands and wives, youngsters and their parents find it very difficult to talk about things that matter.

Talking about deep matters is one of the basic sacramental experiences. The more significant something is, the more difficult it is to bring it to speech. When you bring something to speech, you are bringing it up from the very center of your life. We can paint the parlor at the church with the extremities of the body. But, if we mention the name of

God it comes from the very middle of our lives. Because of this, when we start an evangelism ministry in our church, we have countless people who say, "Isn't there something else I can do? I can mow the church lawn. I can trim the shrubs. I can pass out the bulletins. I can even attend board and committee meetings, but please don't ask me to share my faith with others."

People will say, "I am not a good talker." But, when it comes to the gospel of Jesus Christ there are no "good talkers." As a matter of fact, we probably do not want "slick talkers" trying to represent Jesus Christ. No one should be a glib witness.

Some pastors find it difficult to talk about their faith in Jesus Christ. Many of us would say in all honesty that we have at times been pleased to go visiting and not find the people at home! We leave our card and count that as a visit without having to talk with the people. All of us have heard stories or perhaps been involved in situations where we have been out calling. We were given the name of a specific couple—the Harpers at 513 Fourth Avenue. We drove back and forth in front of the house, and because there were no lights in the front we joyfully assumed that no one was home.

Talking about Jesus Christ is harder than giving money, painting buildings, mowing the lawn, attending committee meetings, and many other important matters that are a part of the life of the church. But, there is a time to speak. Words are important. A true word is a real deed. It builds up life. There comes a time when we must share our faith with others and do so verbally.

There was a mountaineer who lived with his wife deep in the hollows of the Appalachian Mountains. One summer evening the old mountaineer was sitting on the front porch in his favorite rocker. The sun was gently sinking beneath the mountain peak in the west. All the world was turning a beautiful orange. He looked across at his wife of many years. He thought of all she had meant and continued to mean to his life. He thought of the joys and pains they had experienced together.

The man's life was suddenly filled with emotion, but he sat on his hands. He was not good with words. His thoughts became warm and finally he said to his wife, "Matilda, I love you so much, and it is all I can do to keep from telling you." There is a time to say it. The telling is not disconnected from the doing but comes out of the life we live. The hymn says it all: "I love to tell the story; it did so much for me."

In faith-sharing we dare tell what God is doing in our lives. The focus is not on what we are doing for God. Rather, we attempt to witness to the grace of God in our lives. Each human experience of God is unique and valid. Thus, we dare to speak in the first person and share faith. We dare to say, "Christ has done this in my life." Sometimes sharing faith means to share our entire pilgrimage with another. At other times it means to point out some specific experience when God's grace was at work in our lives. Through the networks of neighbor, coworker, family, friend, classmate, colleague, or even the stranger, one can share faith with another.

Faith-sharing comes through personality. Each disciple is called to be a witness. Each has a unique story to share. Sharing faith is as natural and normal as inviting someone to the table. The fact that you are reading this book indicates your interest and desire to share faith with others. You can! And your story matters! There is a gospel according to Matthew, Mark, Luke, and John. There is also a gospel according to George and according to Eddie. There is a gospel according to Mary Nell, Barbara, and Shirley. There is also a gospel according to you. Your witness matters.

A missionary came to speak in chapel during the time when one of the authors[2] was in seminary. As that missionary spoke, he had a globe placed on the table beside him. He talked of the needs of the whole world and each person's responsibility. The missionary then began to talk about the millions of people in the world who could not read. He asked, "What can one person do?" Frank Laubach proceeded to tell how each one can teach another to read. He set in motion a dream and a program. Today there are literally millions around the world who can read because of Frank Laubach's vision. He taught one to read who simply promised that he would teach another.

What a difference one person makes. The witness of each Christian matters a great deal. Each is called to spread the gospel by word and deed. But how do we fulfill our calling?

REFLECT AND ACT

1. How have you experienced God's call in your own life? (See p. 84.)

2. Before reading the chapter, what was your understanding of the function of clergy and the function of laity?

    After reading this chapter, what is your understanding of the role of laity in ministry?

    How does this concept of the role of laity give encouragement and strength to your ministry?

    What will you do consciously and intentionally to claim and act on your responsibility in ministry?

3. List two persons, outside your immediate family, who were important in sharing faith with you. What were the characteristics that affected your life?

4. What are those strengths about your own environment that give integrity to your witness?

5. Share with a friend what God is doing in your life. Talk to someone personally, make a phone call, write a letter.

6. In your relationships this week tell one other person (not family or close friend) what God is doing in your life.

7

Principles for Faith-Sharing

Contemporary church growth research has revealed a number of important facts. Today we know that the process by which people arrive at their commitment to Christ is a key factor in determining whether they become active church members. One study has shown that evangelistic methods can be divided into three main categories.[1]

The first category is called "Information Transmission." This method views evangelism as a one-way act of communicating spiritual facts, dogmas, or propositions. The perceived relationship between the evangelizer and the other approximates that of a teacher and a student. The goal of the transaction is to impart correct information and to secure mental assent. The assumption is that a correct understanding by the hearer (prospect) will result in a logical decision to respond and give mental assent to each "spiritual fact."

Another category is called "Manipulative Monologue." Here the process of evangelism becomes a process of manipulation. Manipulation might center around an emotional appeal or a set of carefully prepared questions to which there are only "yes" answers. The relationship between the evangelizer and the other approximates that of an unprofessional salesperson and customer. The goal of the transaction is to "close the sale."

The final category of evangelistic methods is called "Non-Manipulative Dialogue." This method views evangelism as a two-way process involving honest interaction. It is assumed that no one "canned approach" is appropriate for every situation, simply because different people see things in different ways. Here, the relationship between the evangelizer and the other approximates that of a friend to a friend.

The goal of the relationship is that of sharing love and faith with the other person.

This study discovered that, when evangelism is understood as "Information Transmission," seventy-five percent of those approached will say *No!* Therefore, those who view evangelism as a form of indoctrination realize that they must contact massive numbers of people in order to secure the mental consent of only a few. Among those who practice evangelism as "Manipulative Monologue," eighty-one percent of those approached are apt to say *yes.* However, eighty-five percent of those who say *yes* will become inactive within a year. When evangelism is viewed as "Non-Manipulative Dialogue," ninety-nine percent of those approached will eventually say *yes.* Moreover, ninety-six percent of that ninety-nine percent stay active within the life of the church.

Now, obviously, non-manipulative dialogue assumes an extended relationship between the faith-sharer and the other. Therefore, instead of faith-sharing being understood as a single encounter event, it is understood as an extended relationship that eventually bears fruit. This study indicates that non-manipulative dialogue is the most effective way of sharing faith and bringing people to Christian discipleship. Thus, we see the importance of person-to-person evangelizing.

A second important factor coming from contemporary church growth research is seen in the following statement: More than seventy-five percent of the persons who become Christian disciples do so because of the testimony, deeds, and encouragement of someone they trust.[2] There are three crucial issues revealed in this statement.

First, we understand that effective faith-sharing involves a proper balance of word, deed, and encouragement. Word, here, is understood as proclamation and/or testimony. Deed is understood as faithful Christian lifestyle and service. Encouragement is understood as active initiative on the part of the faith-sharer. The Christian must take the initiative and do as Jesus commanded—"GO." Christians must go to the people, love the people, share word and life with the people, listen to the people, and offer Christ to the people.

This brings us to the second crucial issue. If more than seventy-five percent of the persons who become Christian disciples do so because of the testimony, deeds, and encouragement of someone they trust, then person-to-person faith-sharing must be the highest priority, and we must train our people in this ministry. Christians must be equipped not only with a personal knowledge of Jesus Christ and a knowledge of the gospel; they must also know how to relate to another person in such a way that trust develops.

The third important issue in the evangelizing process is the issue of trust. Trust is the primary basis upon which faith-sharing rests. This raises a very important question: How does one relate to another in such a way that trust develops—trust sufficient to allow one to share how the story of God (the gospel) has intersected one's own personal story or pilgrimage? This is the issue that is most often forgotten in our attempts to equip the people of God for the work of evangelizing.

THE PRINCIPLES FOR FAITH-SHARING

These principles represent a hybrid of our own experience in faith-sharing, our exposure to the writings of Richard Armstrong and Kennon Callahan, and primarily, our learnings from the late Dr. Harry Denman.

Although most of these principles apply to practically every relational encounter, we shall attempt to relate these principles to two basic forms of faith-sharing: (1) faith-sharing within our social networks and (2) faith-sharing with strangers.

FAITH-SHARING WITHIN SOCIAL NETWORKS

Research clearly indicates that more than seventy-five percent of the persons active in church today got their start as Christians and church members through the influence of friends, relatives, neighbors, or colleagues at work. Survey after survey and study after study report that when new members are asked why they chose their church, they respond by pointing to the influence of persons in their social network; i.e., persons within their friendship, kinship, neighborhood or colleagueship network. This is irrevocable proof that **effective outreach is built on relationships.**

We believe that the basic question of human existence is a relational question; i.e., How can a person be properly related to God, the neighbor, the self, and the whole ecological environment? God has revealed the answer to that question in and through the "key event" in all of history: the birth, life, death, and resurrection of his Son Jesus Christ. God's action has made it possible for us to have a personal relationship with Jesus Christ. Since both the basic question and the answer to human existence are relational, it shouldn't surprise anyone to hear that one's ability to establish trusting relationships has an enormous impact on one's ability to share faith.

Research also indicates that the average church member can identify at least six to eight unchurched friends, family members, and associates who live within reasonable distance of their local church.[3]

These realities have led some church growth leaders[4] to conclude that the powerful secret of growth resides in the "extended congregation" which is the cumulative total of the member's unchurched friends, family, and associates living within the ministry area of the local church. Win Arn says, "The members of your 'extended congregation' (normally six to eight times the size of your active membership) are the most receptive people in your entire community to your church and its message!"[5]

The question: How do we reach these persons? The answer: By equipping our members with the skills necessary for the development of trusting relationships and the skills necessary for sharing faith and inviting persons to Christ and his church. Again, let us re-emphasize: **Sharing faith can best take place in a context of mutual trust and respect.** Moreover, faith-sharing within social networks, because it utilizes normal day-to-day relationships, has the potential for the maximum participation of the laity and provides a direct encounter with the larger community. The following principles will aid in the equipping of the people of God for this vital ministry:

1. We Must Be Clear Regarding Our Purpose

It is helpful to divide the purpose into two categories—the initial purpose and the ultimate purpose. Initially, we are involved in a relationship with the other person because we love that person and not because we are trying to change him or her. God brings creative change. God saves and converts. Our initial responsibility is to love the other person even as we have been loved of God. If we approach people in such a way that they perceive we are trying to change them, then we cannot blame them for resisting and backing away.

But faith-sharers have an ultimate purpose as well as an initial purpose. The ultimate purpose can be summed up in the hope that a relationship of trust will develop which is sufficient to allow the sharing of faith and the extending of an invitation. This is done not only out of love for the other but in obedience to the command of Jesus Christ. As ambassadors of Christ, it is Christ's agenda that sets our own. Therefore, it is always our deepest prayer that an opportunity will arise to share faith, to offer Christ, to share the gospel. We are involved in the relationship in order to love, care, listen, serve, share, and invite.

2. Faith-Sharing Must Be Grounded in Prayer

Prayer is the beginning point for every attempt at faith-sharing. The church's involvement and effectiveness in faith-sharing is in direct proportion to the church's prayer life. Our churches are not growing because our members are not praying for growth. Likewise, a Christian's effectiveness in faith-sharing is directly related to the sincerity and intensity of his or her prayer life. The reason for this is really quite simple. Harry Denman stated the reason: "From experience I have learned that when I pray for an individual, or a family, or a nation, I fall in love with that person, or that family, or that nation."[6]

Outreach ministries are always dependent upon the spirituality of the congregation and the spirituality of each Christian who wishes to share faith. The spiritual disciplines of Bible study and prayer are indispensable. Therefore, if we are serious in our attempts to equip our people for outreach, we can never neglect the spiritual formation of our clergy and laity. One of the primary reasons for the growth of the Methodist Church of Korea is the fervency and faithfulness of that church's prayer life. Each morning at dawn the people gather with their pastors and pray earnestly that God will enable them to be faithful witnesses throughout that day and night.

We would offer the following practical suggestions that are enriching the prayer life of congregations:

A. Let us give greater attention to the task of teaching our people to pray. Many of our churches are holding annual prayer conferences which focus upon the development of active prayer ministries. We believe this to be one of the most vital movements in the contemporary church. If you desire information regarding the development of prayer conferences or prayer ministries, please write to: Prayer Ministry Team, First United Methodist Church, 116 N.E. Perry, Peoria, Illinois 61603.

These prayer aids are helpful for the following reasons: First, specific prayer has a way of putting specific persons right at the forefront of our consciousness. Second, we have learned that *if we continue to talk with God about specific persons, we will eventually find ourselves talking with those persons about God.*

B. Let us encourage our people to persist in prayer. Perseverance in
    prayer is clearly taught by our Lord Jesus Christ (Luke 11:5-
    13). Our primary temptation is to give up too easily and too
    soon. Charles H. Spurgeon once said, "Prayer pulls the rope
    below and the great bell rings above in the ears of God. Some
    scarcely stir the bell, for they pray so languidly. Others give but
    an occasional pluck at the rope. But he who wins with heaven
    is the man who grasps the rope boldly and pulls continuously,
    with all his might."[7]

3. Listening Opens the Door for Speaking

There are exceptions to this principle, but they are exceptions and
not the rule. A number of studies have shown that compassionate listening is not only indispensable for all forms of evangelizing; it is itself
a form of evangelizing.[8] Those persons who are not yet Christian both
need and want to be heard. To our shame, we Christians have often
assumed that praying and witnessing consist only of speaking.

Again, Denman insisted that "praying is listening to God." He often
used the illustration of talking on the telephone. "When one person
does all the talking on the telephone, it is not a telephone conversation;
it is a monologue. That is what we have with God, a monologue with
us doing the talking."[9]

In the same manner, we have forgotten that witnessing requires honest, perceptive, non-judgmental, relational listening which conveys trust
and acceptance of the other. Not only is listening a requisite element in
prayer; it is also indispensable for faith-sharing. We will never be effective faith-sharers unless we learn to be good listeners. One of the primary ways of helping people is simply to listen to them.

Some people are so pent-up inside that they desperately need someone to listen to them. Unless we let people have their say, they will be
unwilling to allow us to have ours. We do not know where people are
until they tell us, and listening is the way to learn.

Dietrich Bonhoeffer believed that listening was a form of Christian
ministry. He said:

> *The first service that one owes to others . . . consists in
> listening to them. Just as love to God begins with listen-
> ing to His Word, so the beginning of love for the brethren
> is learning to listen to them. . . . Many people are looking
> for an ear that will listen. They do not find it among
> Christians, because these Christians are talking when
> they should be listening. But he who can no longer listen
> to his brother will soon be no longer listening to God.*[10]

There are three reasons why it is so hard to listen and why there are so few compassionate listeners. First, very few people take the time to pray that God will make them good listeners. How long has it been since you asked God to make you a good listener? It is a prime example of the statement, "You do not get what you want, because you do not pray for it" (James 4:2, NEB). Again, our learning to listen to others is directly related to our learning to listen to God.

In working with clergy and laity, we are encouraging Christians to pray the following "Prayer for Good Listeners." Let us ask God to help us to listen to what is said. Let us ask God to help us discern what is *behind* what is said. Let us ask God to help us hear what is *not* said. In communication, what is left unsaid is often as important as what is said. Finally, let us ask God to sensitize us to needs, concerns, and sad tales.

Second, there are so few compassionate listeners because we forget that listening is a learned art. Someone once said, "That person is a natural-born listener." This is doubtful. Listening does not come naturally. It is born of love for people and it takes time and patience to learn the art. Like most art, good listening comes from repeated practice.

One of the authors is grateful to his wife for helping him see the importance of developing listening skills.[11] The process began shortly after marriage and while serving four country churches. One evening after dinner the author was in the kitchen helping with the dishes. His wife was sharing the events of her day. He was there physically but not mentally. Fortunately, his wife had the boldness to challenge him. She said, "I will not be dehumanized by anyone, least of all my husband. If you do not wish to listen to me, then I will not talk with you."

To be present with another human being is more than mere proximity. We do not listen merely with the ears. We listen with the eyes and with the heart.

Third, it is hard to listen because we are already formulating a response. On the one hand, the mouth tends to outrun the mind. This tendency has given rise to the expression, "running off at the mouth." On the other hand, the mind tends to outrun the mouth. We speak at a rate of 125 words per minute. However, the mind functions with far greater rapidity. Therefore, the mind tends to move ahead of the immediate agenda and fashion the next response. The result is failure to listen to the immediate agenda.

In addition, the mind tends to filter out that which we do not wish to hear or that which might render us vulnerable to the other person.

One professor of evangelism has concluded that there are six rules for good listening.[12] The first is *compassion*. Compassion means to suffer with or to "be with." Compassion is born of genuine love for people. In this respect we are followers of Jesus. Jesus really loved people. He loved his disciples with a compassionate love that survived their slowness to learn and their tendency to let him down. But his love went beyond the twelve disciples. In John 11:3-36 we see how Jesus loved a friend who was outside the immediate circle of the twelve. When the Jews saw tears streaming down His cheeks at the death of Lazarus, they said, "How dearly he must have loved him!"

The love that Jesus had for the poor is amply documented in the New Testament. He came to proclaim release to those in conditions of oppression, poverty, and injustice. Jesus even loved those who rejected him. This can be seen in his call to the rich young ruler and the subsequent rejection. Scripture says, "Jesus looked straight at him; His heart warmed to him" (Mark 10:21, NEB).

Most amazing of all is the compassionate love Jesus showed on the cross for those who put him to death. When he cried, "Father, forgive them; they do not know what they are doing" (Luke 23:34, NEB), he was practicing what he preached to others in his Sermon on the Mount. If we are to follow his footsteps, we are to be lovers first, faith-sharers second. If we do not genuinely and compassionately love people, all efforts at faith-sharing are abortive.

The second rule is *concentration*. This means that we must focus our attention entirely upon the other. Our eye contact must be sufficient to enable us to read body language and to catch nuances of meaning that are expressed by the other.

Third, there is *control*. We discipline ourselves to the point that we know when to speak and when to remain silent. We control the urge to answer every question, as if we knew the answer to every question! It also means that we control our fear of silence. We realize that it is not necessary to continuously fill the air with talk. In human relationships, as well as in our relationship to God, silence is often more productive than speech.

The fourth rule is *comprehension*. This is similar to what the Bible means by discernment, the ability to know where the other is coming from. This is closely tied to our sensitivity to what the other is saying and to what is behind what the other is saying.

Fifth, there is *clarification*. If we are sensitized by the Holy Spirit in terms of our comprehension or discernment, then we can help others clarify their thinking and feeling.

Finally, there is *commitment*. Commitment means that we are willing to stick in the relationship and do whatever love demands. It means that we are willing to enter into an extended relationship with the other.

Harry Denman had only one rule for good listening, but it sums up all that has been said above: "We must never forget that God created us with two ears and one mouth. Surely, God was insinuating that we ought to listen twice as much as we talk."

4. The Christian Witness Is Responsible to Take Both the Person and the Person's Environment Seriously

The important issue of context insists that any strategy for faith-sharing is irrelevant and ineffective if it is not informed by a serious consideration of particular environments. We must always consider the language and the thought forms of the particular people with whom we seek to communicate the gospel.

This is precisely what Jesus did. He consistently used the language and the symbols of the people. He talked about salt and soil, family and festivals, fruit trees and vineyards, kings and servants, shepherds and sheep, flowers and birds, bread and wine. A careful analysis of Jesus' language reveals that he seldom used strictly religious vocabulary.

The revelations of God take place in time and space. The different way in which God spoke at different times is so central in the history of revelation that it constitutes a controlling factor. God does not come to us in a vacuum. God comes to particular persons at particular times in particular places and, usually, with a particular message. Jesus' ministry lends support to this strategy. He started where people were and found a link between their interests and his truth.

The first two disciples to be called were fishermen who were working with their nets. Jesus approached them in terms of their work. Starting where they were, with fishing uppermost in their minds, he said, "Come with me, and I will make you fishers of men" (Mark 1:17, NEB). The woman at the well of Samaria had come there to draw water. Jesus used water as an illustration of the life He could offer her (John 4:7-15).

Moreover, this emphasis upon context is illustrated by Jesus. He approached no two people alike, because no two people are alike. Thus, the evangelistic methods of Jesus were always in tune with the character and situation of the one with whom He had to deal. He had no iron-clad systemized plan of approach. No single religious formula or established precedent was followed by Jesus.

Note that it was only to Nicodemus that Jesus said, "You must be born again." As far as we know, he did not state his challenge that way to anyone else! Why? Because people are not all alike. In other words, as a fundamental principle, the evangelizing of Jesus always takes into account personal history. He knew that every person should hear the good news and see the good news in a language or model that could be understood.

Until this moment appears, the gospel seems void and limited.

People have ears to hear and eyes to see, but this does not mean that they always hear and see. How often it happens that a previously unstruck gospel note goes flying home to people's ears; the moment is right, and they hear for the first time. How often it is that a hitherto unseen aspect of the gospel steps out before their darkened minds; the moment is right, and their whole life is illumined.

The issue of context is also important because people are reflected in their environment. Of all people, Harry Denman was the most sensitive to this fact. He had the ability to discern a person's environment and he was at home in every environment.

If he saw an engagement ring on the finger of a flight attendant, that ring became the basis for a conversation that would enable the young woman to tell about the man she was about to marry, plans for the wedding, and whether the wedding would be held in a church. This would open the door for a conversation regarding the importance of the Christian family. He could spend precious moments relating with corporate executives, and he could spend hours with a housewife rummaging with her through her cupboards, asking about prices, and commenting on packaging. He would spend an evening with a music student, sitting on the floor listening to music and commenting on various records.

Like Paul, Harry Denman was willing to be all things to all people in order that he might share his faith. He cut the cloth of his approach to cover the situation and person which confronted him. He recognized differences in persons and contexts and prescribed his "gospel medicine" with the resourcefulness of a skilled practitioner. However flexible as he was in terms of his manner of relating with people, he was inflexible to the last in terms of his desire to share faith.

5. It Is Better to Make Invitational Statements Than to Ask Questions

Here we do not mean to disparage the technique of asking questions. This technique has been used by many people in a most effective way. Perhaps when a person is learning to share faith, the best way to begin is to ask appropriate questions. However, this technique can become a deterrent to deeper relationships. It is beset by a number of dangers.

One danger is the temptation to memorize a list of standard questions and proceed to ask those questions of every person regardless of context or need. The list of questions may provide a crutch for the witness, but it does not always show sensitivity for the other. Some people use questions as a scare tactic to get people's attention. Those who use this technique can point to some successes. However, only God knows how many times this approach has not only failed but has served to build resentment in the other.

Pastors and laity alike can fall into a trap if they have memorized a standard list of questions. There is the tendency to ask those questions of every person, whether calling in a hospital, factory, or home. In some situations, the idea of responding to questions can make the other feel victimized by a style of psychological nosiness.

Therefore, we encourage clergy and laity to move beyond the technique of asking questions to making invitational statements. *An invitational statement is a statement of fact or an observation which has the "seed" of a question within it.* The employment of this technique may be awkward at first, but it is more productive in the long run.

This technique demonstrates a higher degree of sensitivity. It assumes that in relational faith-sharing there are signs that say, "By Invitation Only." It acknowledges the fact that we are not only, at times, guests in someone's house, but likewise, in faith-sharing we are essentially guests in someone's life. As guests, we proceed only by invitation. Trust develops as the witness is invited into the other person's life. An invitational statement gives the other person an opportunity to take up the invitation and move the relationship forward, if desired.

One of the authors[13] will never forget Marshall (not his real name) and his excruciatingly painful journey to a living faith in God. Like some others, Marshall entered Candler School of Theology not so much because of his commitment to Christ or his surrender to the call to ministry but rather in hopes that he might discover a relationship with God. He was not brought up in a Christian home.

During Marshall's senior year in college, a fraternity brother invited him to participate in a work mission with the Appalachia Service Project. For the first time in his life, this son of well-to-do parents "smelled the stench of poverty." He found himself asking deep questions about life. "What is the meaning of it all?" "Is there a God?" So, he shocked his parents with the announcement, "I'm going to seminary."

For reasons known only to him, Marshall enrolled in the author's evangelism course. After the first two weeks of classes, he came by the office and announced he was quitting school. In response, the author said, "Apparently you have already discovered what you came here to find." (Notice this is an observation and not a question.)

"No, I have not!" Marshall retorted. "I will never find it in this place. People here are too busy to spend time with me." The author promised to "stick with him through thick and thin." This was the beginning of many dialogue sessions.

Finally, the turning point came in Marshall's spiritual and academic journey. After completing about half of his seminary curriculum, he came by the office one day. It was before Valentine's Day and he had in his hands a large, red, heart-shaped box of candy which he intended to send his mother. The author said, "Well, Marshall, it looks like you're finally getting to the heart of the matter." (Notice this is not a question. However, the seed of a question is within the statement.)

Surprisingly, he blurted out, "O God, what is the heart of the matter? All of my life I've been bombarded with all sorts of philosophies and ideas. What is the center, the heart of it all?" The author said, "Marshall, are you ready—really ready—to hear this? Do you really want to know?"

He replied, "Is the Pope Catholic? Of course, I do!"

The author said with conviction, "Jesus Christ is the Son of God, the Lord of creation and Savior of the world. By God's grace he can be your Lord and Savior too. That, dear friend, is the heart of the matter. Believe that with all your heart and you will have found the answer to your quest." We spent a time in prayer and Marshall made his discovery. He went on to complete his seminary training and is now one of the finest pastors in the southeastern United States.

The time has come when we need to train our laity and clergy to make invitational statements rather than to lean upon a standard set of questions.

6. If People Volunteer Information, We Can Rest Assured They Wish to Tell Us More

This depends upon our willingness to allow them to do so. For example, assume you are sharing with a person and notice a picture of a lovely young woman on the mantel. She is in her wedding dress. You say to the mother, "That is a lovely young woman."

The mother responds, "That is Doris. She is our youngest. She was married eighteen months ago, and you know, she and her husband moved off to Akron, Ohio, and we have not seen that girl in eighteen months."

Now, if we have been listening, we will hear some of the loneliness, disappointment, and hostility of this mother, who feels neglected by her youngest daughter. You can almost hear her saying, "After all we've done for that girl, you would think she could at least come to see us once in awhile!"

What does the witness do with that loneliness and hostility? If we thump our Bible and say, "Well, the Bible says . . . ," we will probably end the relationship right there. Most sidetracking transpires in human relationships right at this point. Some sidetracking happens unconsciously. Witnesses find themselves saying, "We certainly have been having terrible weather!" The witness must decide whether to become vulnerable to this lonely mother. We must ask ourselves: Are we willing to share her pain? Can we handle it?

Actually, there is only one appropriate response to this woman's anguish, and that is to say, "It really is difficult to be absent from our loved ones." Then, the witness must prepare to listen carefully as this mother tells just how tough it is. If people volunteer information, they wish to tell us more if we will let them.

7. To Do the Mission of Christ, One Must Have the Mind of Christ

Philippians 2 contains what scholars have labeled the "Kenotic" hymn. The word *kenosis* is a Greek word which means "emptied." The passage reads:

> Let the same mind be in you that was in Jesus Christ, who, though He was in the form of God, did not regard equality with God as something to be exploited, but emptied Himself, taking the form of a slave, being born in human likeness. And being found in human form, he humbled Himself and became obedient to the point of death—even death on a cross (Phil. 2:5-8, NRSV).

This means that Christian mission or witness is a matter of the mind as well as heart, soul, and strength. In faith-sharing we must constantly pray that we might possess the mind of Christ. We are not saying that faith-sharing requires a "great" mind. We are saying that it requires the "right" mind. We all know that it is possible to have a "great" mind without having the "right" mind. Without the mind of Christ, the witness tends to get off track and is driven by motives that are not appropriate. Without the mind of Christ, we tend to pander to people's selfish wants without addressing their fundamental needs. As a matter of fact, *we cannot discern the mission of Christ or the needs of others without the mind of Christ.*

Thus, the faith-sharer constantly prays, "Let the same mind be in me that was in Christ Jesus." Christ Jesus made himself vulnerable to people's basic needs.

8. It Is Better to Expose Our Vulnerability Than to Pretend Invulnerability

The word *vulnerable* comes from a Latin word meaning "to wound." It means capable of being hurt or open to pain. Thus, to be vulnerable is to open one's life to the possibility of sharing another's pain. It also means facing up to our own woundedness, our own shortcomings.

Vulnerability requires an incarnational self-emptying of anything that would separate witnesses from the persons with whom they wish to share the gospel. Any expression of superiority by which the witness condescends in relating to people is a denial of the Incarnation. Jesus made this identification in his birth, baptism, and death.

If the "pioneer and perfecter of our faith" (Heb. 12:2, NRSV) felt it necessary to render himself vulnerable, how much more necessary for us? We all stand amazed at the beautiful humility of our Lord. He was no snob. His point of contact with people was in his common humanity. This teaches us that faith-sharing goes wide of the mark if it is done in the spirit of "pity for the heathen" or even with a hint of arrogance or condescension. The Christian witness must never pretend invulnerability.

Harry Denman's attitude and lifestyle were typical of this Christlike vulnerability. His favorite request was, "Pray for Harry Denman, a sinner saved by God's grace." He made that request of every sort of person imaginable. Denman made no secret of the fact that he frequented bars and liquor stores. As a traveling man he knew that some of the loneliest people on earth could be found in motel and hotel bars. Once while attending a denominational board meeting, he found one of the authors[14] in the hotel lobby late one evening.

He said, "Let's go fishing." We went into one of the hotel bars. It was obvious that Denman wished to relate to the barkeeper. Therefore, he positioned himself down at the end of the bar.

The barkeeper came down to our end and said, "May I help you?" Denman put forth his hand and said, "As a matter of fact, you can. My name is Harry Denman and I desperately need your prayers."

Startled, the barkeeper asked, "What did you say?"

Denman repeated his statement verbatim.

Puzzled, the barkeeper said, "Sir, I am afraid you've come to the wrong place."

Denman probed, "You mean you can't pray for me?"

The young man paused a moment and said, "Sir, I can't even pray for myself. How can I be expected to pray for you?"

With mercy, Denman responded, "You mean you can't even pray for yourself?" Conviction settled upon that handsome young man. It was as if his life suddenly paraded before his eyes. He became aware that he had strayed so far from God that he could not pray for himself. Before we left the bar, Denman had that young man's home address, knew the name of his wife and their anniversary date, and the name of his child. He used that information to keep up a steady stream of correspondence and materials.

Denman's tapes from workshops on witnessing show why he was willing to render himself vulnerable to others. He said that it afforded four precious freedoms.

First, you are free to abstain from arguing. He was convinced that even if you win the argument, chances are you have lost the person. For that reason, he never argued with people. Arguing is often an attempt to render oneself invulnerable to the other.

Second, his own vulnerability gave him the freedom to stand on the same ground with prisoners, barkeepers, waiters and waitresses, tenant farmers, taxi drivers, business executives, the whole world. As one rendered vulnerable by the grace of God, he knew that he did not have to pose as an authority on religion.

Third, this vulnerability gave him the freedom to say those three little words, "I don't know." He knew that people were not really interested in our infallible answers to complex questions. He listened with compassion but he refused to argue, and he knew that he did not have to have the final answer to everything.

Finally, this gave him the freedom to believe that one does not have to be an expert in order to witness.

9. God Is Far More Interested in Our Availability Than Our Ability

In the final analysis there are no "experts" when it comes to faith-sharing. Now, there are those who think they are "experts"! However, "experts" tend to trust too much in themselves and in their method. Their tendency to feel self-sufficient is a carbon copy of Adam's mistake.

Always our faith and hope must be grounded in what God, through the power of the Holy Spirit, can do in spite of our weaknesses. Regardless of how personable and polished the witness perceives himself or herself to be, the scriptures indicate that self-confidence can be misplaced confidence. We are admonished to deny the self rather than push the self front and center.

Our experiences in faith-sharing in various parts of the world have taught us again and again that faith-sharing is not simply what we do, but something God does through us. If we make ourselves available— so does God! **We have learned that no matter how well trained we are in certain methods of evangelism, our witness will be unproductive without the blessing and power of the Holy Spirit.**

Our primary challenge is to make ourselves available and open to the Holy Spirit. When we are fully available and yielded, we experience the "Acts 1:8 sequence." You receive power when the Holy Spirit gives power; power enables witness; witness results in outreach. Thus, without the Holy Spirit we lack power; without power we fail to witness; without witness there is no outreach.

If we truly make ourselves available, God will enable us to overcome the challenges of limited speaking ability, limited courage, and limited power.

But, what do we say when we have earned the right to share faith?

10. We Do Not Tell People Why They Should Believe or What They Should Believe. We Tell Them Why and What We Believe

The Holy Spirit uses this approach to break down resistance in people and make them receptive to the good news of Jesus Christ. The manner in which we attempt to communicate affects the receptivity of the other person. For instance, if we manipulate people in such a way that they judge us as trying to tell them *what* they ought to believe and *why* they ought to believe it, then we build resistance in people. People will either brush off the approach or else they will apply emotional filters.

Soren Kierkegaard's principle of indirect communication is helpful. As pastors of several local churches, the authors followed the procedure of having moments with the younger church. These moments usually consisted of a simple Bible story or illustration. The little children were invited to come forward, and we were seated together in the chancel area. After the service was over, and while greeting the people in the narthex, adults would often shake the pastor's hand and say, "Pastor, I get more out of the children's story than the sermon." Having spent hours crafting that sermon, such comments were disappointing.

However, Fred Craddock, preacher and teacher, helps us understand what was happening.[15] The children's story is a form of indirect communication for adults. The children were brought forward and the story was directed to them, which enabled the adults to lower their defenses just long enough to "overhear" the gospel.

Another illustration of indirect communication can be seen in the phenomenon of the "hospital ward." On many occasions pastors have visited people in multiple-bed hospital rooms. Usually the curtains between the beds are pulled. While attempting to share faith with a particular person, suddenly the pastor hears someone else weeping behind the next curtain. The fact that communication is directed toward person "A" enables person "B" to lower resistance long enough to "overhear" the gospel.

This same dynamic is present when Christians give a testimony. After relating with another in such a way that trust develops, the freedom is available to tell the other why *we* believe and what *we* believe. The fact that we are sharing our own personal faith enables the other to lower resistance long enough to "overhear" the gospel. It is for this reason the Holy Spirit uses the personal testimony with such great effect.

Moreover, this is why all Christians must understand that they have a story to tell and the responsibility to tell it. All of us, all of the time, ought to be looking for opportunities to tell how God's story in the gospel has intersected with our own personal pilgrimages and stories. When this good news is shared within a relationship of trust, power is unleashed, the Holy Spirit is at work, and lives are transformed.

11. Witnessing, Therefore, Is Most Effective When Done in the First Person

It is better to make "I" statements than "you" statements. That is, one does not say, "You ought," or "You should." Instead, say "For me," or "In Christ I have" or "With Jesus, I know."

FAITH-SHARING WITH STRANGERS

We must recapture the viability and vitality of person-to-person faith-sharing with strangers. In order to highlight this need, we have decided to focus on one specific model of faith-sharing with strangers: house-to-house visitation.

At one time this form of evangelizing was very common. However, today this is not the case. Lyle Schaller has identified at least a dozen reasons why house-to-house visitation no longer works. In its place he recommends direct mail.[16] For the most part, churches have abandoned this model of faith-sharing. To a degree, this is understandable, but we believe the time has come to take another look at this time-honored method.

Luke teaches that the early apostles "did not cease to teach and proclaim Jesus as the Messiah and they did this in the temple and from house-to-house" (Acts 5:42, NRSV). In this passage we find the Greek word *euangelizomenoi* which means they evangelized or proclaimed Jesus as Messiah. Little attention is given to the fact that this was done from house-to-house. In fairness, the New Revised Standard Version does include "house-to-house" but only as an alternate reading.

Without a doubt, John Wesley certainly knew the importance of house-to-house visitation. Wesley knew that the Wesleyan Movement would stagnate and decline without consistent person-to-person contact and vigilant visitation. He knew that visitation was an arduous chore; nevertheless, he did it faithfully. In his journal he wrote: "I reached Colchester. I found the Society had decreased . . . and yet they had had full as good preachers; but that is not sufficient. By repeated experiments we learn that though a man preaches like an angel, he will neither collect nor preserve a society which is collected, without visiting from house-to-house" (Dec. 29, 1758).

In 1774 he wrote: "I began at the east end of the town to visit the Society from house-to-house. I know no branch of the pastoral office which is of greater importance than this. But it is so grievous to flesh and blood, that I can prevail on few, even of our preachers, to undertake it" (Jan. 12, 1774). The historic ordination questions asked of all clergy in the Wesleyan Tradition include the following: Will you visit from house-to-house?

Unless our pastors and laity are committed, motivated, and trained to move outside our cozy church gatherings and walk the streets, dusty roads, highways, and the marketplace where people live, our denomination will continue to decline in membership and spirituality. The constant infusion of new Christians into our fellowship is required to keep alive the spiritual vitality which characterized that early apostolic church, described in the Acts of Apostles, and that early Methodist Movement which spread around the world.

Admittedly, faith-sharing within social networks is the most effective form of outreach. However, it has its limitations. The fact that most Christians have within their primary network mainly other Christians means that there are perhaps millions who will not be reached by the gospel without an intentional strategy to encounter the stranger. House-to-house visitation is a viable way of accomplishing this.

The following principles are especially relevant for house-to-house visitation. We trust the reader will observe that these principles are consistent with the incarnational-relational approach followed throughout this book and expressed in the eleven principles necessary for Social Network Witnessing.

As in every form of faith-sharing, house-to-house callers must be ever more willing to love and to listen, because the goal is always to start and build an ongoing relationship. In an outstanding chapter, Kennon Callahan highlights the need for callers who have the capacity to share friendship and a longing to assist with specific human hurts and hopes discovered in their visits.[17] Therefore, the first eleven principles also apply to house-to-house calling. What follows are very specific details and key principles that have been discovered by practitioners of house-to-house visitation.

1. Sensitivity to the Other Person Begins Before You Ring the Doorbell or Knock

In house-to-house visitation the issue of context begins as the visitor remains sensitive to territory and space. For instance, when we knock on the door, it is best to step back two or three steps. If we stand too close to the stranger, this tends to raise anxiety. If there are steps leading up to the door, it is helpful to move down two or three steps. As visitors, this deliberately puts us on the lower level and makes our presence less threatening to the other.

This important principle cannot be overstated because many people have opened their door to someone and have confronted a judgmental attitude and an arrogant spirit on the part of the visitor. Perhaps you have seen the cartoon that pictured two men standing at the door which has been opened by the homeowner. "Hello," they say. "We're here to quote the Bible and make you feel like scum! May we come in?"

That cartoon sends shivers through the hollow laughter of those of us who really love people and are sensitive to them as well as their territory and space. Since God did not send his Son into the world to condemn it (John 3:17, NRSV), neither does he send Christians into communities for that purpose.

2. In Establishing a Relationship with a Stranger, the Introductory Moments Are of Crucial Significance.[18]

What we say, our manner of saying it, our posture, and our attitude will either enhance or annul the possibility of an extended relationship. It is impossible to make the first impression a second time. In doing house-to-house visitation, we desire to get inside the house. Moving from the front doorstep into the house greatly enhances the possibility of an extended relationship. Whether we are invited inside depends upon how we handle the introductory moments.

In the introductory statement it is always best to focus upon relational rather than functional dynamics. Many potentially productive relationships are nullified because the visitor focuses on functional dynamics in the introductory statement. Here is a typical example: "Hello, my name is Reverend John Smith, pastor of Morning Star United Methodist Church. I understand you are new in our community, and I thought I would drop by on my way to the hospital and welcome you to our community." Several aspects of this introductory statement are inherently damaging to an ongoing relationship.

First, there is the obvious preoccupation with the self. It is always better to start with the other than to start with the self.

Second, there is disregard for the fact that newcomers to a community are ordinarily self-conscious about being "new." Of course, they realize that they are "new," but they do not wish to be reminded by strangers standing on their own doorstep.

Third, the statement sets up a damaging "us-them" dichotomy. It divides people into insiders and outsiders. People like to feel they are a part of the community.

Finally, this functional statement treats the other person as an after-thought. It insinuates that the other is not worthy of prime time in the visitor's schedule. Functional statements deter friendly relationships.

The following is an example of an introductory statement which is sensitive to relational dynamics. This statement has six parts and each is important in enhancing a relationship with a stranger:

A. **Give a friendly greeting** ("Good afternoon sir/madam"). If the other is a stranger, this is a helpful way to begin the relationship. For a number of years one of the authors[19] tried to make the greeting more personal by learning the name of the stranger from a neighbor next door. Thus, before leaving house "A" he learned the name of the neighbor in house "B." However, he encountered enough resistance to this method that he no longer uses it. In today's world, if a total stranger walks up to your doorstep and calls you by name, there is a tendency to spend the next five to ten minutes trying to figure out how this total stranger knows your name. Rather than enhancing the "getting-acquainted" process, this tends to sidetrack it.

B. **Make known your identity** ("We are the Smiths from Briarcliff Church"). The secret of identification is to say enough without saying too much. Therefore, it is better to give a community label to your church rather than a denominational label. If the denominational label is put forth prematurely, the other will use it as an opportunity for a favorite sidetracking device. That is, the other will say, "Oh, well, we are Baptists." Sometimes this means that a great, great grandmother was a Baptist! At any rate, it is important to identify who you are. Ordinarily, in North America people are accustomed to having only two types of religious visitors: Mormons and Jehovah's Witnesses. The fact that people think of religious visitors only in these categories is a terrible indictment of mainline denominational churches. Fundamentally, it says that we are no longer willing to go to where the people live. Rather, in our pride, we expect the people to come to us.

C. **Explain why you are there** ("Good afternoon sir/madam, we are the Smiths from Briarcliff Church, and we are calling on our neighbors in the community"). After trying many different remarks, we find this to be the best one. Rather than setting up an "us-them" dichotomy, this statement draws a circle that includes the other.

D. **Acknowledge the intrusion** ("Good afternoon sir/madam, we are the Smiths from Briarcliff Church. We are calling on our neighbors in the community. We hope this is not an inconvenient time for you and your family"). This statement acknowledges the fact that when we ring someone's doorbell uninvited, more than likely we are intruding in the life of that person and/or family. To acknowledge the intrusion is to register our own human sensitivity. This helps the other person to realize that we are sensitive, honest human beings.

E. **Ask to come in** ("We hope this is not an inconvenient time for you, but we would love to visit with you and your family. May we come in?"). Years ago both authors, while participating in the Summer "E" Programs in Salt Lake City, Utah, and El Paso, Texas,[20] had an opportunity to work with Harry Denman in house-to-house visitation. Denman noticed how reluctant some of us were to ask the people to enter their houses. He said to us, "Whose feet took you up to their doorstep? Whose finger rang the doorbell?" We said, "They were our feet and it was our finger." He replied, "Then, the ball is in your court." He reminded us that we often fail to get inside the house simply because we fail to ask. "We have not because we ask not."

F. **Promise to be brief** ("We would love to visit with you and your family. May we come in for a few minutes?"). Experience teaches that the initial visit in a home tends to follow a "bell curve." Normally, the visit will begin at the bottom of the curve and build in quality until it reaches a peak. However, the visitor must be sensitive to the fact that the relationship can start down the other side of the bell curve rather rapidly. This is especially true if the visitor overstays his or her welcome. It is important to leave when you perceive the relationship to be at its peak. The reason is your desire to visit in that home again. You really wish to feel welcome in that home. If you wait until the visit starts "downhill," the chances of being welcome again are not good.

Careful attention must be given to the crucial significance of introductory moments. In working with clergy and laity, it is necessary to have them play the roles several times through the introductory remarks. However, we caution you to avoid memorizing a formula. The goal is to establish fruitful ongoing relationships.

3. The Encounter Is Not a Waste of Time Even If We Are Not Invited Inside

A number of significant things can be accomplished without being invited into the home.

For instance, with rare exceptions, we have found it appropriate to ask the other about church affiliation. It is best to put the question as follows: "What local church do you and your family attend?" If we put the question in general denominational terms, this makes it much easier for the other to sidetrack the question.

Second, if we ask to come in and do not get a positive response, it is good to immediately reach for our date book and say, "Is there another time when it would be convenient for us to visit?" It is helpful to always carry a date book. This tells the other that we are willing to go out of our way in order to establish a relationship.

Third, we can always hand out an attractive program brochure. Each local congregation needs to give careful attention to the production of an attractive brochure. The smaller the church, the greater the need for an attractive program brochure. In a culture that equates size with success, people tend to look at small church facilities and assume that they are not offering very much in the way of creative ministries.

Finally, the most helpful statement is to simply say, "Sir/madam, is there any way in which our congregation can serve you and your family?" This is a disarming comment which helps the other understand that we are not out soliciting, but offering our love and service.

4. In House-to-House Visitation There Is Even Greater Need to Take Personal and Contextual Factors Seriously

Harry Denman was a master at putting people at ease and respecting important aspects of their environment.

When he walked into a home, he was always conscious of the presence of children. He acknowledged their presence and spent time with them. If there were no children present in the home, he would look about the room for pictures of people. His comments on these pictures often became the basis for a growing relationship.

In house-to-house visitation, when entering a home, consciously survey the environment. When you begin this discipline, it is very awkward. Later, the process will come naturally. It is very much like learning to drive an automobile. When we begin the experience, we grip the steering wheel furiously and we can only see that portion of road immediately in front of us. However, after we learn to drive, we begin to relax and develop a panoramic vision which allows us to be sensitive to a much larger environment.

In one home, one of the authors[21] was invited into the front room and sat on a large couch. At one end of the couch, beneath a lamp, there was a picture of a lovely child. He commented, "What a fine young man!" The man of the house replied:

> *"That's Buster! You know, Ma and I have seven grand-children, but there's something special about ole' Buster. Now mind you, I would not make that statement to just anybody, but there's something special about that boy. Do you know what he does? Why, you can set your watch by that boy. Every afternoon when he gets off the school bus, he comes by here to check on Meemaw and Beepaw!"*

In establishing growing human relationships, these kinds of comments are the essence of life. After that comment, it was easy to talk with this mountain couple about our loving God.

More and more we notice an absence of pictures of people in homes. This is especially true in urban and suburban areas. Maybe this is a sign of the dehumanization and the depersonalization of our secular society. However, we must learn that just as it is important to take people as they are, it is likewise important to take them where they are. Therefore, we need to take seriously whatever we find in their environment.

For instance, during house-to-house visitation among affluent people in a large city in Australia, one of the authors[22] noticed an enormous painting on the living room wall:

"Now that's an interesting piece of work."

The man of the house said, "Oh, you like that, do you, mate? Do you have any idea why we bought that particular painting?"

The Holy Spirit does supply our needs in these moments when we are put on the spot: "Well, it is obvious that it perfectly matches the color scheme in your draperies and carpet."

The lady of the house said, "Oh! You notice that, do you!" She continued, "But, that is not why we bought the painting." She then went to the opposite side of the room and gave the following instructions, "Squint your eyes and as you look at the painting, do not concentrate upon the dark portions; rather, concentrate upon the light portions."

Well, the author did his best and suddenly saw what looked like a dove: "Is it a dove?"

She exclaimed, "You're the first one to ever see it!"

This couple told that they bought this particular painting because they were a part of the Australian peace movement. They had just returned from Perth, where they had participated in a demonstration against a United States nuclear-powered warship that had docked in Australian waters. When the moment was right, the author said, "You know, the Bible has several beautiful stories about the dove."

The man of the house said, "Well, we are not religious people. We know nothing about the Bible."

His wife retorted, "That does not mean that we do not wish to know. Would you tell us those stories?"

It was a remarkable opportunity to tell the story of Noah and how the dove brought the olive branch as a sign of new life and hope, then about the baptism of Jesus and how the Holy Spirit descended upon him as a dove. This became an opportunity to share faith with these people and to offer Christ, the Prince of Peace, to both of them.

On the other hand, one of the authors,[23] while pastoring a "store-front church" in a city ghetto, discovered that no matter how impoverished the people or how poor the dwelling, there was always some picture or calendar on the wall. These often became bridges for conversation which led to deeper relationships in which faith was shared.

Harry Denman also taught the wisdom of paying careful attention to furniture, especially old furniture. As he once said, "Remember, behind every old piece of furniture there is a family story." This is quite true, and if we can enable a person to tell the family story, this offers an opportunity to share the story of Jesus. The Christian witness takes both the person and the person's environment seriously.

Another way to take a person's environment seriously is to take careful note of what the other has in his or her hands.

On a plane out of O'Hare Field one of the authors[24] sat beside a young executive. He had the look of success all over him! He was reading a copy of *Playboy* magazine and was so intensely interested that he paid absolutely no attention to anyone. He was sitting on half of the author's seatbelt, and the author had to literally pull it from beneath him. The man paid no attention to this movement. Without looking, he merely lifted one-half of his body in order to free the other half of the seatbelt.

What a tremendous challenge to engage this person! The title of the article in *Playboy* had to do with a religious census that had been taken in the United States. Apparently, the article was commenting on this

census and giving views as to whether the Christian faith was gaining
or losing in its influence.

After a time, the author turned to him and said, "My, that looks like
an interesting article." (Notice, this is a statement of fact, not a question.
However, the seed of a question is within the statement.)

Reluctantly, the man looked up and said, "As a matter of fact, it is
very interesting. The article says that mainline denominational churches
are losing membership and influence and that only Pentecostal and
sect-type churches are growing." He paused for a moment and continued,
"As far as I am concerned, I don't give a damn about any of that."
He raised his eyebrow a bit and said, "Do you want to know what I
think about the matter?"

By then the author was conscious that all of the people seated
around were intensely interested in this conversation. He replied, "I
would be most interested in hearing your views."

He took up the cue and said, rather bombastically, "I am convinced
that by the year 2000 only a tiny handful of people will even remember
there was such a person as Jesus Christ."

The author replied, "Well, if I were you, I would not hold my breath
and wait for that to happen."

He retorted, rather angrily, "Well, what gives you the right to make a
statement like that?"

The author observed, "You see, Jesus Christ is alive, and it is almost
impossible to forget people who are alive. They impinge themselves
upon you."

With a quizzical look, the man said, "How do you know Jesus Christ
is alive?"

A Christian witness could not ask for a better opportunity! The
author told him the story of his own encounter with Jesus Christ. It
was an amazing opportunity to do proclamation in a public arena. The
time has come when we need to train our laity and clergy to make invitational
statements rather than to lean upon a standard set of questions.

These are the principles that guide us in sharing the faith. But how
do we help persons claim faith for themselves?

REFLECT AND ACT

1. In the next two days pray each morning and evening that God will enable you to be a compassionate listener. Pray during the day as you engage in relationships that you will be a compassionate listener.

   Reflection: How has this impacted your listening and your relating to persons?

2. Make a list of the seven or eight persons in your social network—friends, relatives, neighbors, or colleagues at work or school—who are outside the fellowship of the Christian church.

3. This week make at least one attempt to share faith with someone within your social network, using the principles outlined in this chapter.

4. This week make at least one call on a person whom you do not know, using the principles outlined in this chapter.

   Reflection: Were you faithful to the principles?
   Were you comfortable?
   What were the positive responses and factors?
   How could you improve the call?

5. Two of the principles relate to taking a person's environment seriously. Next time you go into an office, a gas station, a home, pay special attention to the environment. What were the pictures, the signs, the context? Were you open to be able to hear and see and feel the environment? What did it say? How did you use that context to relate to that person?

6. Practice invitational statements in your everyday relationships with family and friends. What difference does this make in your relationship?

7. You may want to select one other person to go calling with and to share with regarding your faith-sharing for encouragement, support, and prayer.

Inviting Persons to Receive Christ

O f all the issues involved in faith-sharing, inviting persons to receive Christ is most often feared, abused, and misunderstood. Thus, many pastors and laity back away from this crucial aspect of Christian witnessing. The authors, in travels throughout the church, have received many requests for help with this concern.

No responsibility is more important in the ministry of sharing the good news of Christ than helping a person in the process of receiving Christ. This responsibility is approached with great care and sensitivity. When a person is seeking God and needs help with coming to faith, this enabling ministry is a great privilege and joy to the Christian witness.

In the process of sharing faith, the closure of an encounter with another person depends on four factors: the leadership of the Holy Spirit, the faith-sharer's assessment of the quality of the relationship, the degree of receptivity on the part of the other person, and the context. These four variables seem to be present in every faith-sharing situation.

The context or arena has a great influence upon the manner of closure. For example, if you are sharing with someone on a plane, and that person is getting off in Nashville while you are going on to Chicago, the manner of closure is limited. But, contextual limits have always affected witnessing.

As we saw in the chapter on the arena for faith-sharing, the varieties of contexts in the New Testament influence the varieties of ways in which people discovered faith in Jesus Christ. Thus, we see a difference in the faith experience of the travelers on the road to Emmaus and Paul on the road to Damascus. There was the blazing light which struck Paul blind. His encounter was sudden and dramatic. However, the ones who travelled on the Emmaus road eventually realized the Lord had been with them all the time.

The encounter of the woman at the well was different from the Ethiopian eunuch. She was dramatically confronted by Christ with the offer of living water. She met the Messiah where she least expected to see him. The eunuch, however, was searching the scriptures without understanding them. He needed someone to explain the message. He was a seeker after truth, and Phillip introduced the Messiah. The faith-sharer must always be sensitive to the arena and environment.

Second, it is imperative that we assess the quality of the relationship. Has the other person shown a willingness to open up and trust us? Very closely related to this dynamic is the faith-sharer's perception of how receptive the other person is. Has the person shown interest in the message conveyed? Have needs been expressed that indicate receptivity and a seeking on the part of the other?

Finally, and most important of all, the manner of closure depends on the leadership of the Holy Spirit. In the final analysis, only the Holy Spirit can sensitize us to the *kairos* moment—the moment pregnant with possibility and grace. The witness tries to always remain open to the leadership of the Holy Spirit and obedient to the guidance of the Holy Spirit.

THE SEEKER

There are those times when persons are ready to respond in repentance and faith. The Spirit has been preparing them to be receptive. The message of the gospel has been shared, and it has penetrated their existence. There are times when persons recognize their need for God. They may not phrase it that way, but the recognition is there. It may be expressed as a desire to discover life or to know a sense of meaning. The relationship with the faith-sharer may have been brief, or it may have been a series of encounters over a longer period of time. But the person is ready and asking, "What shall I do?" This person is ready to receive Christ.

Bryan Green calls this person a seeker, one who has moved along the pathway and is now "seeking a decisive moment when his/her faith in Christ may be certain and real in experience."[1] The Christian faith-sharer is called to help at this point. The seeker wants God as a living reality in his or her life. We can be sure that God desires this as well. As Green points out, God does not intend that "people should go on and on seeking and never finding. 'Seek and ye shall find,' are the words of Jesus."[2]

GUIDELINES FOR INVITING

Many persons come to this faith experience without direct words of counsel, but for most (e.g., the Ethiopian eunuch) a caring counselor and interpreter makes the difference. Jesus' story of the seed growing secretly highlights this process. The farmer sows the seed. The seed grows and bears fruit. As soon as the crop is ready and ripe, the farmer applies the sickle. As we said earlier, a faith-sharer needs to be alert to this time of harvest. Just as certain as the seed is scattered on the land, there will be a time of reaping. The farmer is alert to the time of harvest and, at the appropriate moment, applies the sickle. There are principles to guide us in sharing faith in Christ, and there are also guidelines to help us in inviting persons to receive Christ.

1. **The invitation flows out of the nature of the gospel.** The gospel discloses a living God who is forever inviting people to respond. Therefore, we invite persons to say *yes* to God because God has already said *yes* to all people. Christ "is the *yes* pronounced upon God's promises, every one of them" (2 Cor. 1:20, NEB). It is appropriate to invite people to say *yes* to God. Therefore, we invite persons to receive Christ.

2. **The human response consists of turning and trusting.** We invite persons to turn away from sin and bondage and toward God and salvation. The possibilities of repentance and faith are gifts of God, but the decision to exercise faith and turn to God is a conscious act on the part of the human being.

3. **There are many methods of inviting persons.** There is a tendency to find only one way of inviting persons and to insist that everyone come that way. As we emphasized earlier, we do not have a programmed tape inside to play on command. We share the good news of Christ with the hope and prayer that persons will respond in repentance and trust. Although the responses of persons will vary, it is the reality of the experience of the living Christ which is paramount.

4. **In inviting persons to receive Christ, we do not pressure people but take pressure off people.** Remember, the faith-sharer is not required to convert anyone; only God can do that! In this way, the faith-sharer is a part of God's gracious concern for all people.

5. **The faith-sharer is sensitive to life's important intersections.** A person is lost in a strange city. She needs to be on Interstate 40. Finally, she sees the appropriate road, but there seems to be no way to enter it. She asks for help regarding the road. The service station attendant tells all about the road. "Oh, so you want I-40—it is a wonderful road! You can travel all the way across the country on it. At times it is four lanes wide, but at other places it is ten lanes. It is concrete in one place, but at others it is asphalt. It is a wonderful road!"

   This is not what the woman needs! She needs someone to point out the entrance to the road. Inviting a person to receive Christ can be an entrance ramp. We can help a person in the time of discovery. The invitation is a means of enabling a person to respond in faith because an intersection of decision is pointed out by the faith-sharer.

6. **The faith-sharer offers the invitation with clarity.** We attempt to make the invitation as explicit as possible. We do not deceive people. We are forthright. We endeavor to help them see how God meets their specific needs now. We point out what is involved in this act of faith.

7. **The faith-sharer offers the invitation with integrity.** We do not manipulate persons. The manner and method in which the person is invited to a commitment of trust is under the judgment of the gospel of Christ. We are honest in the process of leading a person to faith in Christ.

8. **The invitation to respond in faith is a community affair.** It is necessary to help people see that they are not alone in the search for faith. We are all part of a community of faith which encourages us and holds us accountable. This support helps us grow and develop as disciples of Christ.

9. **In inviting a person to receive Christ, one must be willing to wait in expectant hope and humility for a response of faith.** We respect a person's integrity and response. If a person says *no*, we assure the person of our genuine love and concern. Thus, we respect the sacred right of rejection. If a person says *yes*, we are willing to help that person on the journey of faith.

10. **The faith-sharer trusts the Holy Spirit.** We endeavor to be sensitive and alert to the movement of the Spirit. As we have indicated again and again, this is the most critical guideline in every facet of faith-sharing.

CLOSURES

Here we offer a variety of ways for inviting response, knowing well that the manner of closure is dependent upon the variables and guidelines listed above. If the encounter has been a brief one, merely a time of getting acquainted, then it is important that you leave in such a manner that the budding friendship can eventually blossom. Just as the encounter begins with the other, it is important that it end with the other. Therefore, make no excuse for leaving. Never say, "I must be going. I've got a busy day." That insinuates that other things are more important than the person with whom you have been visiting.

Rather, it is helpful to say, "Mary, I have really enjoyed our time together and look forward to seeing you again." By leaving in this manner, you have left the relationship open and invited the relationship forward in the desire that it will move to a deeper level.

Second, if you sense that the other has expressed an interest in the church, you might invite him or her to attend very specific worship services or events in your congregation. It is better to give invitations to specific occasions rather than the general invitation, "We would love to have you visit our church." For instance, it would be better to say, "Our Koinonia Sunday School Class meets next Sunday morning at 10:00 o'clock. It is a friendly group of people and all of us would enjoy having you in our fellowship. I would be happy to be there to introduce you to some friends." Next, if the relationship has revealed specific needs, you might explore with the other person possibilities of how your church can respond to those needs.

Finally, if you sense that it has been a faith-sharing experience, and if you feel the leading of the Holy Spirit, offer the person an opportunity to receive Christ or to reaffirm his or her faith in Christ.

INVITING THE SEEKER

As the Holy Spirit works in the life of the faith-sharer and in the life of the other person, there comes a time when a person is interested and open to the invitation of Christ. The following is a graceful pattern for sharing the good news of Christ and assisting persons in receiving Christ as Lord and Savior. This <u>grace</u>ful pattern can be illustrated by the points of the "Bethlehem Star."

A GRACEful Pattern
for Faith-Sharing

G = *God's Grace in Christ Jesus for All*

- God's grace in creation
- God's grace in redemption
- God's grace in hope and eternity

Helping a person become aware of God's grace for *all* people and of God's continuing desire for a relationship of wholeness with humanity and creation is a significant step toward establishing a relationship with God. God created this world and said that it is good. God's grace in Christ is seen in creation:

> In him (Christ) all things in heaven and on earth were created, things visible and invisible (Col. 1:16, NRSV).

The image of God is stamped in the creation of humans:

> God created humankind in his image, in the image of God he created them (Gen. 1:27a, NRSV).

It is through grace that persons discover their worth as created by God. Our esteem is rooted, therefore, not in self-esteem but in grace-esteem. During the Wesleyan revival across eighteenth-century England, people responded to the incredible good news that God's grace is for all. Albert Outler points to this central affirmation, "The heart of Wesley's gospel was always its lively sense of God's grace at work at every level of creation and history in persons and communities."[3]

God's grace is seen in creation and in the providence of God. By the graceful gift of God in creation, human beings are given a conscience which enables them to discern good and evil. However, human beings rebel against the sovereign rule of God and are alienated from God. This estrangement results in bondage and the corruption of creation. Therefore, all humans are in need of salvation and are unable to save themselves. This salvation comes by grace through faith. A key understanding for the faith-sharer and a key discovery by the seeker is that:

> By grace you have been saved through faith, and this is not your own doing; it is the gift of God—not the result of works, so that no one may boast. For we are what he has made us, created in Christ Jesus for good works, which God prepared beforehand to be our way of life (Eph. 2:8-10, NRSV).

Again, helping a person discover that God's grace is for all (even me) is a major step toward "being saved."

R = *Recognizing and Repenting of Our Sin*

- Receiving salvation in Christ
- Responding in trust
- Reconciling Grace, being put right with God through the atoning blood of Jesus Christ in his death and resurrection.

Helping persons recognize the reality of sin and its resulting bondage is an important step toward repenting (turning away from) of our sin. It is out of a profound sense of need that people cry out to the God of grace. Our basic alienation is the result of endeavoring to live without God. Bryan Green quotes Archbishop Temple regarding the reality of sin: "The alienation of (humankind) from God is a fact. It is not our business to deny it but to end it."[4]

The tragedy is that we have not become what God in creating us intended us to be. Wesleyan Christians believe the image of God was damaged, defiled, distorted, and disfigured because of sin, but not totally destroyed. A very significant step to responding in trust is the realization of our sin and the subsequent repenting of our sin. The recognition of our inability to redeem ourselves leads to a response of faith in God's saving love which is rooted in the atoning death and resurrection of Christ Jesus.

A = *Accepting of God's Forgiveness*

- Acknowledging Christ Jesus as Lord and Savior
- Assurance through the witness of the Holy Spirit
- Awareness of the continuing grace of God

Helping persons come to accept God's forgiveness of sin is a very important part of the process of being saved. Through Christ, the grace of God is accessible to all. Indeed, the heart of the gospel is:

For God so loved the world that he gave his only son, so that everyone who believes in him may not perish but may have eternal life (John 3:16, NRSV).

The work of atonement (at-one-ment) made possible through the life, death, and resurrection of Jesus Christ is for the whole world. Through acceptance of this grace, we can know forgiveness of sin and experience the restoration of the image of God in our lives.

It is very important to relate the gift of grace in Christ Jesus to specific needs, great or small, which the seeker raises. The faith-sharer helps the seeker discover the reality of Christ in meeting specific needs. Here the faith-sharer may need to interpret and envision how God does meet our deeply felt needs. That is, it is very helpful for the seeker to envision what it would be like if Christ came into his or her life.

Closely related to helping the seeker take this step of acceptance is helping the seeker to experience the assurance of being in a right relationship with God. Here the Holy Spirit bears witness with the human heart that we are forgiven. Through the Spirit, love lives in our hearts and is reflected in our lives. Through the witness of the Holy Spirit, we can know that we are accepted by God. Here we are reminded of the moving testimony of John Wesley on May 24, 1738, in a prayer meeting on Aldersgate Street in London, England:

> *About a quarter before nine, while he (the leader) was describing the change which God works in the heart through faith in Christ, I felt my heart strangely warmed. I felt I did trust in Christ, Christ alone for salvation: and an assurance was given me, that he had taken away my sins, even mine, and saved me from the law of sin and death.*[5]

Persons receive joy and assurance as they experience the reality of the work that God is doing in them.

> When we cry "abba! Father!" it is that very spirit bearing witness with our spirit that we are children of God (Rom. 8:16, NRSV).

The faith-sharer can help the seeker come to the assurance of a right relationship with God. Assurance may come suddenly or gradually. The reality of this experience of salvation is rooted in the goodness and graciousness of God. Our faith and trust is in the faithful, living God who has fulfilled all the promises made to us. The faith-sharer helps the seeker know this assurance.

C = *Confessing Faith in Christ Jesus*

- Committing in trust to Christ Jesus
- Commencing the way of Christ
- Continuing the walk with Christ

In order to appropriate the benefits of Christ's atoning work of grace, each person, by faith, must confess Christ as Lord and personal Savior. Though God's saving grace is intended for all, it is not irresistible. We are created in the image of God with freedom of choice, and God will not violate our nature, even to save us. We cannot redeem ourselves, but neither can we be saved without ourselves. God alone is the giver of grace and salvation, and by the grace of God we may choose to accept the gift of salvation. Or we may refuse to accept the gift when it is offered.[6]

The faith-sharer helps a seeker confess faith in Christ Jesus. We seek to help persons put trust in Christ (John 3:6) and receive him (John 1:12). People must be encouraged to put their trust and confidence in God.

There comes a time in the faith-sharing process when the seeker is invited to say *yes* to the invitation of Christ. Faith-sharing is similar to the sacrament of Holy Communion in that there comes a moment after the bread is broken and the cup is lifted and the invitation given that one takes and eats the bread and drinks from the cup. The faith-sharer needs to be highly sensitive to this *kairos* moment when a person is ready to say *yes* to Christ. This act of faith commences a journey with Christ.

E = *Entering into the Reign of God*

- Entering into the fellowship of the Church
- Entering the way of the grace-filled life
- Entering into the mission of God

The witness encourages and assists the seeker in the process of entering the reign of God and the community of faith. Throughout this book we have consistently focused upon the central message of Jesus Christ:

The kingdom of God. Even as our Lord yearned for Nicodemus to both "see and enter" the Kingdom (John 3), we humbly confess that we share this yearning. As we said earlier, "If people hear the gospel and under the inspiration of the Holy Spirit, trust the good news of Jesus, they convert; that is, they repent or turn around. They switch kingdoms." They become Kingdom people.

In order to be faithful to the Kingdom, they need the support of others. Thus, support given by others is important in the making of disciples, and it is indispensable in order that the person continue faithfully in Kingdom living. John Baillie once said, "I cannot be a Christian all by myself. I cannot retire into my shell or into my own corner and live the Christian life. A single individual cannot be a Christian in his singleness."[7]

A part of the New Testament understanding of conversion involves incorporation into a local church.[8] To misconstrue conversion as an isolated, individualistic experience without any reference to the local community of faith is to do irrevocable damage to the biblical concept of Christian conversion. John Wesley once said, "To turn Christianity into a solitary religion is to destroy it."[9] God wills not only a new person but a new community, a community of celebration, mutual support, serving, and witnessing. Christ's invitation to conversion is immediately followed by his call to discipleship. To offer conversion without incorporation into the life of the church is to set people up for a fall.

According to the New Testament, awareness of one's individual identity before God necessarily involves one in community. Life in the Spirit of Christ is the life of new openness to others in a fellowship of reconciliation. This teaches us that the individual's new personal identity as a Christian is formed through identification with Christ in his Body, the Church. Therefore, a part of the evangelistic call is to turn from independency, self-sufficiency, and pride that characterizes human beings in their individualism and to submit to the Lordship of Jesus Christ within his community, the Church.

So, the biblical pattern is not a detached individual savoring his or her own private religious experience. It is, rather, new creations in Christ who necessarily involve themselves in responsible participation in our Lord's Church. Membership in the Church of Jesus Christ as part of a congregation is essential. Therefore, we should never be hesitant to encourage new Christians to join a congregation of believers.

It is not our purpose here to attempt an extensive examination of incorporation into church membership or membership care and cultivation. This emphasis is found in other books. However, we insist that decision for Christ must lead to discipleship—and that means responsible membership in a community of faith.

An important part of the faith-sharer's responsibility is to help the seeker realize that the same grace which makes possible the response of trust is also given to enable us to grow fully into the stature of Christ Jesus. As a trusting recipient of the grace of God, we are filled by grace and become a person full of grace, or a grace_ful person.

SAVED BY GRACE

The process of being saved by grace through faith leads to a new life in Christ Jesus (2 Cor. 5:17, Eph. 2:8-10). Again, let us review the process which leads persons to put their trust and confidence in God:

- **G** od's grace in Christ Jesus
- **R** ecognizing and repenting of sin
- **A** ccepting God's forgiveness
- **C** onfessing faith in Christ Jesus
- **E** ntering the reign of God and the Church

In knowing God's grace and being aware of need, the seeker must respond. This response is a conscious act of the will. God is present with people, but people must will to be present with God. The key words are to desire and be willing to receive the new life in Christ. Scripture focuses this time of decision:

> Listen! I am standing at the door, knocking; if you hear my voice and open the door, I will come in to you and eat with you and you with me (Rev. 3:20, NRSV).

> But to all who received him, who believed in his name, he gave power to become children of God (John 1:12. NRSV).

The seeker is called to trust the Lord and accept the divine invitation. With deep humility the faith-sharer invites the seeker to say "I will" to the Lord. The witness helps the seeker see that he or she can enter into this new relationship with Christ *now*. If the seeker is not ready to say *yes*, the faith-sharer indicates his or her understanding and love, and assures the seeker that God will continue seeking. If the seeker is ready, there is nothing more appropriate than prayer.

Like our mentor, Harry Denman, we believe that people are "prayed into the kingdom." Again and again he said, "What we need to do is to get people to pray."[10] For this reason he continually asked others to pray for him.

We have discovered that it is more fruitful to make the prayer uplifting, i.e., make the prayer a matter of praise. For instance, we might pray the following:

> *Dear God, we thank you for the gift of your love in Jesus Christ. We praise you for taking the initiative and reaching out to us through Jesus Christ. We are grateful that you loved the world so much that you gave your only Son that whoever believes in him should not perish but have eternal life. We praise you for making it possible for us to have our relationship with you restored. We are grateful that, through the death of your Son, you have dealt with the problem of sin which spoiled your image in us and our relationship with you. We thank you for offering us the gifts of forgiveness and new life.*
>
> *And, dear God, we are especially grateful that you have brought our (brother/sister) to this moment of commitment and decision. Surely your goodness and mercy have followed (him/her) revealing your love to (him/her) in a very special way. We praise you, we adore you. We give you thanks that you have brought (him/her) to this moment of confession and surrender. We know that your Holy Spirit will make (him/her) become the kind of person that you want (him/her) to be. We thank you for your undeserved kindness and we know that you will enable (name of person) to continue to grow in (his/her) love for you and care and concern for others.*
>
> *Now, we pray that you will help (name of person) to understand that the Christian life is a partnership. We praise you that we are not expected to struggle in our own strength and power. We praise you for the gift of your Holy Spirit bringing us new power to live everyday. We also praise you for the gift of other Christian sisters and brothers and for the support they give us in our Christian journey. Now, we pray that (name of person) will open (his/her) heart and invite you to take charge of (his/her) life.*

At this point it is helpful to take the sister or brother by the hand (depending on the leadership of the Holy Spirit, we might lay our hands upon his or her head) and pray the following prayer based on Ephesians 3:14-15:

> *(Name of person), may the Creator strengthen you through the Holy Spirit in your inner being; that Christ may dwell in your heart through faith, and that you may be filled with all the fullness of God.*

Then, we usually ask the new convert to pray a simple prayer of thanksgiving. If he or she appears to have difficulty with this, we very gently and tenderly offer to help with a thanksgiving prayer. For example:

> *Dear God, I thank you that you love me and know me. I have sinned. I have tried to live by my own strength. I have not followed your will for me. Thank you deeply that while still a sinner Christ Jesus died for me. By your grace I repent and turn from my sin and by your grace I accept your forgiveness. By your grace, I confess Jesus Christ as my Lord and Savior. Through the power of the Holy Spirit, enable me to live a faithful life in your Kingdom. In the name of Jesus Christ. Amen.*

All five points of the "graceful star" are important in the process of sharing faith. All are a part of the star's total brilliance. It is important to remember that the points make up the whole.

The pattern offered here does not have to be carefully followed step by step in sequence. Our desire is to point out the various aspects involved in a response of faith, and to help the faith-sharer be used by the Holy Spirit in inviting a person to receive Christ.

As we share faith with others, there will be those times when a seeker is ready to receive Christ. We know of no greater joy than that of being present when a sister or brother appropriates faith and receives Christ. Jesus said, "I tell you, there is joy among the angels of God over one sinner who repents" (Luke 15:10, NEB).

Let us share the faith and the joy! But, sharing faith is an awesome responsibility. Where do we find the strength and power for such a task?

REFLECT AND ACT

1. If you have not already prayed a prayer of confession and commitment, or if this is an appropriate moment for rededication, perhaps you would like to, in prayer, commit your life to Christ or rededicate your life to Christ.

2. In your relationships with persons in the next two weeks, try inviting persons to Christ. Mark those steps you will take in these next weeks, in each setting, being sensitive to the four variables (p. 115).

   ❏ I will invite someone to a specific event related to the church, and offer a ride or to meet outside, to help that person get to the right place with a friend.

   ❏ I will invite someone who is not involved in outreach ministries to come with me to participate in meeting a specific need.

   ❏ I will relate to someone over a period of time and be sensitive to his or her receptivity.

   ❏ I will invite a person to respond to God's love and forgiveness, to receive new life in Christ.

   ❏ I will invite someone who is not active in the church to come home with me after church and will share my faith.

   ❏ I will make two calls on persons and invite them to new relationship to Christ and the community of faith.

3. See the "graceful star" on page 120. List the points of the star. Recite the word G-R-A-C-E. Looking at the choices you have made in suggestion #2, reflect on where persons were in this process as you shared faith and invited persons. How were you responsive to the suggestions in the chapter relating to inviting? What have you learned that will help you in the future?

9
The Power for Faith-Sharing

W e are not only called to be sharers of the good news of Jesus Christ; we are given the power to do this ministry. This is incredible good news. Jesus promised his disciples that power would be given them to fulfill his ministry and mission in the world.

The promise of Jesus, just before his ascension, makes clear the relationship between the Spirit and the power for witnessing.

> You will receive power *when* the Holy Spirit comes upon you; and you will bear witness for me in Jerusalem, and all over Judea and Samaria, and away to the ends of the earth (Acts 1:8, NEB).

There is a direct correlation between the Holy Spirit and faith-sharing or witnessing. One can witness only after the Spirit comes. Without the Holy Spirit, there is no Christian witness. Evangelist Alan Walker of Australia often tells about the race of the sailing yachts in which Australia defeated the United States for the prized America's Cup. For 132 years the cup was kept and defended by the United States. Again and again there were challenges for the cup, but each time it was retained by the United States. Finally, in 1983 Australia mounted a serious challenge. The event took place as scheduled, and after six races, the two yachts were deadlocked at three wins each. Now the whole world seemed to take notice. Australia was alive with anticipation. The sporting world was focused on the race. The day came for the final race. After more than 100 years, the United States was in danger of losing its very precious cup. Thousands of people came to watch the race. Television cameras were ready to beam the race by satellite around the world. The crews were ready. The boats were polished. The yachts pulled into place at the starting line. All was ready, but there was *no race*! There was not enough wind. In yachting, no wind means no race!

The word in the Old Testament which is translated "Spirit" is the word *ruach*, which literally means "wind" or "breath."[1] In the New Testament, Jesus talked to a religious leader about the wind and the Spirit (John 3). The Spirit is *like* the wind which blows as it wills. The wind is absolutely essential for a yachting race. The Holy Spirit is absolutely essential in the life of the witness or faith-sharer.

The Book of Acts points to this reality. Before the Spirit came, the disciples were despondent, discouraged, and afraid. When the Spirit came, they were energized, encouraged, and empowered. These ordinary men and women became flaming witnesses for Jesus Christ and the kingdom of God. The story in Acts is the story of a Spirit-empowered church just as the story of Jesus is one of a Spirit-empowered ministry.

Jesus began his ministry by announcing, "The Spirit of the Lord is upon me" (Luke 4:18, NRSV). The story of the early church begins with the words, "When the day of Pentecost had fully come" (Acts 2:1, NRSV). The promise of power which Jesus made was fulfilled at Pentecost. The power of the Holy Spirit was the power for ministry. Just as certain as "no wind means no race," so "no Spirit means no witnessing." Therefore, one who desires to share the good news of Christ must be filled with the Holy Spirit. The Holy Spirit is absolutely essential in the ministry of faith-sharing.

THE HOLY SPIRIT ENERGIZES

The Holy Spirit is the energy in the life of the Christian and the community of faith. The Spirit enables one to be filled with a passion to witness. Those early disciples waited in Jerusalem to receive the Holy Spirit and the power from above. When the Spirit came, the disciples had to witness. There was a dynamic source of energy let loose in the community of faith and the lives of the disciples. The Spirit is like an engine to an automobile. Can you imagine trying to race a car which has no engine?

Recently a friend, who was the former chairman of the board of the famous Charlotte, North Carolina, Motor Speedway, invited one of the authors[2] for a ride around the track in a race car. With tremendous power the car surged to over 150 miles per hour for one lap after another! Such a race would not be possible if the car were missing an engine.

It is just as certain regarding the presence of the Holy Spirit in the life of the community of faith. For one to attempt to function in the life of Christian discipleship without the Spirit is like trying to take a trip in an automobile without an engine. The Spirit is the internal combustion that releases an energy which gives us both a compulsion and a compassion to share faith in Jesus Christ.

There is a mystery here. In Acts, the coming of the Spirit is "like that of a strong driving wind, which filled the whole house . . . And there appeared to them tongues like flames of fire" (Acts 2:2-3, NEB). The Spirit is like wind and fire. A little girl said to her grandfather, "What is the wind?" The grandfather replied, "Darling, I don't know, but we can lift a sail." The Spirit is not under our control. The Spirit comes to us not because of our goodness, but because of God's graciousness. The Holy Spirit is let loose in the world. We respond by opening our lives to the Spirit. The Spirit is the source of our energy for faith-sharing.

THE HOLY SPIRIT GUIDES

The Holy Spirit is the guide in our faith-sharing. The Spirit enables us to stay on track in our witnessing. We share faith in Jesus Christ. We point to Jesus Christ. We introduce persons to Jesus Christ. This is the particular ministry of the Holy Spirit. In the Gospels, there is a continuing, explicit reference to the Holy Spirit in the life of Jesus. Jesus was conceived by the Spirit (Matt. 1:18, Luke 1:35), baptized by the Spirit (Matt. 3:16, Mark 1:10), filled with the Holy Spirit (Luke 4:1), led by the Spirit (Luke 4:1), and armed with the power of the Spirit (Luke 4:14). He then went to his hometown synagogue and announced, "The Spirit of the Lord is upon me" (Luke 4:18, NRSV). The Spirit was seen as operative in the ministry of Jesus.

Thus, the very content of the Holy Spirit is found in the character of Jesus. Jesus linked the ministry of the Spirit with his ministry. Again and again he made it clear that the Spirit would come to "glorify me" (John 16:14). Jesus declared that "the Holy Spirit, whom the Father will send in my name, will teach you everything, and remind you of all that I have said to you" (John 14:25-26, NRSV).

The Holy Spirit enables us to know who Jesus is. The Holy Spirit comes to enable persons to know Jesus and to become like Jesus in character. When the Spirit comes, the Spirit guides and directs our lives after the life of Jesus. The Spirit guides our witnessing, enabling us to stay on course. In addition, the Spirit leads and directs us in our living. Any action which is out of step with the character of Jesus is not being prompted by the Holy Spirit. The Holy Spirit is the guide for faith-sharing. The Spirit glorifies Jesus Christ. Again, Jesus said, "When the Holy Spirit comes upon you . . . you will bear witness for me" (Acts 1:8, NEB).

THE HOLY SPIRIT MOTIVATES

The Holy Spirit comes to motivate the disciple of Jesus and the community of faith. The disciple is given the power of the Holy Spirit to do ministry in the name of Jesus.

A man was always repairing his car. He was asked if he was going on a trip. "No," he replied. "I am not going on any trip. I just want my car to run well and idle smoothly." This is not the picture of a disciple of Jesus. We are not given the Spirit to enable us to operate smoothly or to idle well. The Spirit is given to put us in motion in the ministry of offering Christ to the world. The Spirit enables us to dare risk-sharing faith. The Holy Spirit makes us willing to fail! The Holy Spirit gives a holy boldness to ordinary people.

Simon Peter was a living example. Only days before Pentecost he denied even knowing the Lord. When a young girl accused him of being a disciple of Jesus, he denied it. He was even afraid to admit that he was a Galilean. But after Pentecost, notice the difference. He was empowered to speak in the name of Jesus. His fear was overcome. The same power of the Holy Spirit is available for Jesus' disciples today.

The Holy Spirit enables our faith to be alive. The Old Testament prophet Ezekiel had a vision of a valley of dry bones (Ezekiel 37). The Lord came to the prophet and asked him if he saw the dry bones. The Lord further inquired of the prophet if he thought the bones could live. The prophet answered, "You are the Lord; you ought to know." The Lord spoke, and the bones began to connect together, and flesh grew on them. Again the prophet was asked, "Can these flesh and bones live?" Again the answer, "You are the Lord; you should know." Then the Lord breathed into the flesh and bones the breath of life; and they came alive! The bones and flesh became living beings—leaping, serving, and praising the Lord.

The Spirit comes to raise us from the dead and motivate us for faith-sharing. A living faith in the Lord constrains and compels us to share the gospel with others.

THE HOLY SPIRIT PREPARES OTHERS

The Holy Spirit is active in the lives of all people. Another incredible word of good news is that the Spirit precedes any attempt to share Christian faith with others. The Spirit is manifested as the prevenient grace of God in all people. The Spirit awakens, arouses, disturbs, convicts, and convinces persons of their need for God even while they are alienated from God. Notice the clear work of the Holy Spirit at Pentecost. The Spirit enables persons to "hear and understand" the good news in their own language and experience. It is the Holy Spirit that enables human beings to hear the Word of the Lord and repent. Thus, the Spirit is the active agent in the new birth (John 3).

It is important for the witness to know that God's Spirit strives and seeks persons long before the attempt to share faith. This has a positive impact upon the attitude of the faith-sharer toward self and the other. God's grace and Spirit given for us means that we are important and of great value. God's grace and Spirit seeking the other means that all people are valuable and significant in God's kingdom. It is the Holy Spirit who fills the faith-sharer with compassion for other persons, and it is the Spirit who draws people to Christ.

FITNESS FOR FAITH-SHARING

Sharing faith demands that we remain open to the Holy Spirit. The key is to continually yield our lives to the Spirit. This involves spiritual diet and spiritual calisthenics. Without proper diet and exercise, fitness is impossible. Just as we must be committed to working out in order to develop physical fitness, we must be committed to developing spiritual fitness in order to grow as disciples of Christ. As Leander Keck states, "Plowing does not make it rain but does make it possible for things to grow if it rains."[3] There are appropriate ways to prepare for the indwelling of the Holy Spirit. Wesley refers to these ways as the means of grace. The diet or means of grace for spiritual fitness includes:

- Studying the Holy Scripture
- Worshiping and regularly receiving the Lord's Supper
- Christian fellowship or small groups
- Prayer and fasting

For John Wesley these means of grace are ordained of God. Through them God conveys to persons both grace and power. Wesley did not believe that these means were the only way God bestows power upon us, but they are specific ways and means by which God does work. These means are channels of the grace of God, enabling and empowering us to live as faithful Christians and strong witnesses for Christ.

First, the faith-sharer *studies faithfully the Holy Scripture* in order to get the story straight and to become a mature disciple. An ongoing systematic study of the Bible is needed as much as food in order to serve in the name of Christ.

The Faith-Sharing New Testament, developed by the authors, can be a helpful tool in this study. This resource emphasizes the importance of using the Bible as the primary source of one's learning and testimony. The section in front of the Gospel of Matthew offers the faith-sharer basic training in the nature of Christian conversion and discipleship. The section following the Book of Revelation focuses on the essentials for leading a person to Christ. Both sections are keyed to relevant passages in the New Testament as well as to relevant chapters in the *Faith-Sharing* textbook.

The faith-sharer must *participate in worship* with the body of Christ, the church. All who desire to grow in grace and power will avail themselves of the holy sacrament of the Lord's Supper. Power flows through this channel of grace.

Third, every Christian needs to be a part of a *Christian fellowship* or small group in order to grow and be empowered for living and witnessing. Here the faith-sharer receives the support and encouragement necessary for the Christian journey. The small group enables the faith-sharer to be accountable in terms of service and witness in the world.

Finally, *prayer and fasting* is a necessary ingredient in the diet and exercise of the faith-sharer. Jesus expected his followers to pray and fast. Note that he said, "*When* you fast" (Matt. 6:16), not *if* you fast. John Wesley urged Christians to fast and pray. For more than fifty years, Wesley followed a systematic pattern of prayer and fasting. He would take no solid food after the evening meal on Thursday until mid- to late afternoon on Friday. For him it was not a long or sacrificial fast, but a regular and frequent fast which enabled him to focus his prayers. The World Methodist Conference in Singapore in 1991 passed a resolution which encouraged persons to follow this "Wesleyan pattern" of prayer and fasting. Hundreds of thousands of Wesleyan Christians are regularly engaged in this pattern.

The life of prayer includes both solitude and solidarity with others. This is not an option if one desires to receive the power of the Holy Spirit. The early church met together in one place, and they "were constantly at prayer together" (Acts 1:14). "Stay in the city," Jesus said, "until you are clothed with power" (paraphrase, Luke 24:49). "Wait," said Jesus. Jesus had promised the Spirit, and they were expecting it.

So today the Christian does not wait in vain. The Spirit always comes to the community of faith gathered in the name of Jesus. The Spirit gives to the community of faith the inner power and resources to carry out the ministry of witness in the name of Jesus. The presence of the Holy Spirit in the life of the witness means that the faith-sharer is never alone. The amazing promise is that the Spirit is here now for the empowerment of God's people.

Glenn "Tex" Evans was truly a remarkable witness for the Lord Jesus Christ. He gave his life in ministry among poor people in the southwestern United States, Hawaii, and southern Appalachia. He told a story of a man in the church he pastored which makes clear this message of God's presence. Hear "Tex" tell it in his own words:

When I was a student in the university I had a student charge, a beautiful little Methodist church in a quiet community, and I had the privilege of living in the parsonage while my sweet wife and I took care of that little church. We had three delightful years there, and any other preacher will understand that no church is ever quite as magnificent and remarkable as one's first church.

Now this church had very few people, but those it did have were indescribable in their kindness and friendliness and helpfulness to one another, to their neighbors, and to this preacher and his wife.

One other thing in that church which was due for special mention and recognition is the teacher for our adult Sunday school class, a Baptist saint named T. T. Gentry! He was a retired school teacher from Oklahoma and was in love with life. I am sure that the children who had him for a teacher found themselves blessed in more ways than one can count.

Brother Gentry loved the soil and the creatures of the forest—birds and bees and rabbits and squirrels— almost as much as he loved people. One of his choice loves was poetry!

Brother Gentry could quote poetry by the hour. Most of his poetry was from English poets and the early American poets, of course! His favorite poet was Longfellow. He could quote Longfellow for a while but after getting around to certain beautiful, moving passages, Brother

Gentry could not go on. His emotions would get the best of him. When he could catch a vision from one of Longfellow's poems, such as "A voice fell, like a falling star, [said] Excelsior!" Brother Gentry just could not control his tears because of the beauty and power of the poetry.

All this I say just to indicate the kind of man he was.

One day, I was talking with another fellow up the street and he said to me, "Tex, did you ever go up to see Brother Gentry in the daytime?" When I assured him that I had, he said to me, "Well, did you ever notice that he has apple trees and bee hives, and a rose garden, and a vegetable garden, and a regular flower garden?" When I assured him that I had noticed, he had another question, "Well, did you ever notice that no matter what he's doing, whether he is in the rose garden or taking care of his bees, or working with his apple trees—no matter what—he is always whistling?" I allowed that I had noticed that Brother Gentry did whistle!

Then, my friend reminded me that he didn't even whistle a tune. He just very loudly whistled with a sure steady whistle changing from one pitch to another so as to give some variety, I suppose, to the exercise. Then he had another question for me. "Now, do you know why he whistles?" When I admitted that I did not, as a matter of fact, know any reason for his whistling, he had a suggestion for me. "Well, the next time you are over there, and he is whistling, you look on the front porch and you will see why Brother Gentry whistles."

Now I could hardly wait! On Tuesday I came home as early as I could from the university, parked my car, and told my wife that I had to go up and see Brother Gentry about something. And, I did!

I went walking briskly down the little street toward his home, and before I got right up to his house, I could hear him in his rose garden whistling away in his slow, firm tone, changing the pitch from this to that as he constantly whistled. When I walked up, Brother Gentry looked at me, paused, raised his hand, and said, "Come on over, and I'll give you a rose!" He had on rather rough gloves. He had some little snippers in his hand and was trimming some of his roses. I walked up close to Brother Gentry, paid him brief courtesy, and asked him how he was getting along and quickly looked toward the front porch.

There on the front porch sat Mrs. Gentry. She was in a wheelchair, and she was blind! Brother Gentry was whistling for Mrs. Gentry! He wanted her to know that he was there. He wanted her to know that she was not alone. He wanted her to know that he was mindful of her and that he would not leave her, that he was available, that he would come to her.

Now I went home from that meeting having been enriched immeasurably. I had seen something entirely beautiful and lovely and true. And I said to myself, "God is like that. He knows about us; he is concerned for us. He is aware of his children; he will not leave them. Our Father will not desert his children. Our Father will come to us!"

I will not make any long application of this beautiful truth. I will just comment that I am constantly astonished at the folk who are so caught up with complaining and whining and fear and doubt and worry — and they have been within walking distance of the Christian faith all their lives! They ought to be right in touch with immeasurable sources of love and light, with meaning and power and hope. In these brief words I would just like to remind the reader that you are not alone. You are loved. Our Father knows. Our Father cares.

Our Father will not go away and leave us. We will not be deserted. He will come to us.

So, as we begin any new day we might very well say, "Well, this may be a pretty rough day but I can at least count on this: Our Father is whistling all the time!"[4]

God is like that. The Holy Spirit is the living presence of Christ among us and in us. We are not left alone in this life of Christian discipleship. God comes to us. Christ lives within us. The Spirit is present with us.

Again, we reiterate the ministry of the Holy Spirit in the process of faith-sharing: (1) The Holy Spirit comes to inspire the faith-sharer; (2) the Holy Spirit moves in the life of the seeker in prevenient grace; (3) the Holy Spirit enables the seeker to hear the witness; (4) the Holy Spirit enables the faith-sharer to witness; and (5) the Holy Spirit makes possible the response of repentance and trust by the seeker.

The bottom line is this: The power of the Holy Spirit is the power for faith-sharing. Let us be about this joyous responsibility.

> *Sometimes I feel discouraged,*
>   *And think my work's in vain,*
> *But then the Holy Spirit*
>   *Revives my soul again.*
>
> *There is a balm in Gilead,*
>   *To make the wounded whole;*
> *There is a balm in Gilead,*
>   *To heal the sin-sick soul.*
>
> *If you can't preach like Peter,*
>   *If you can't pray like Paul,*
> *Just tell the love of Jesus,*
>   *And say he died for all.*[5]

REFLECT AND ACT

1. When and how have you experienced the Holy Spirit in your life, empowering, compelling you to witness?

2. In this week, pray for the power of the Holy Spirit in your life for witnessing.

3. Read the following passages: Acts 8:26-40, Acts 9:10-19. Who sent? What was the message? Who was the messenger? How did God prepare the recipient?

    Why did each of the messengers go? Have you ever experienced inner urgings to call or write or go somewhere? When? Did you or do you see that as being sent by God, as the promptings of the Holy Spirit?

    Reflect in this week. Have you been open to the promptings of God's Spirit? Have you responded? How? What difference did it make for you or for another?

4. When have you experienced yourself as dry bones? (p. 134, Ezekiel 37). How have you known the power of God's Spirit bringing you alive once more?

5. When have you experienced yourself in life to be as Mrs. Gentry, blind, in darkness, immobilized? When and how, in those moments, have you experienced the living presence of Christ?

Endnotes

CHAPTER ONE

[1] Fox.

[2] Loren Mead, *The Once and Future Church* (Washington, D.C.: The Alban Institute, 1994), p. 10.

[3] Paul Scherer, *The Word God Sent* (New York: Harper and Row, 1965), p. 25.

[4] John Newton, "Amazing Grace," *The United Methodist Hymnal* (Nashville: United Methodist Publishing House, 1989), 378.

[5] Francis Thompson, "The Hound of Heaven" (first published 1893).

[6] Leander E. Keck, *Mandate to Witness* (Valley Forge, Pa: Judson Press, 1964), p. 71.

[7] Fox.

CHAPTER TWO

[1] L. Harold Dewolf, *The Aim of Evangelism* (Nashville: Methodist Evangelistic Materials, 1965), p. 21.

[2] Alan Walker, *The New Evangelism* (Nashville: Abingdon Press, 1975), pp. 9-12.

[3] Walter J. Burghardt, S.J., "Life—And More Than Enough," in *The Living Pulpit* (July-September 1995), p. 4.

[4] Martin Luther, *Lectures on Romans* in *Luther's Works*, Vol. 25, p. 466.

[5] George E. Morris, *The Mystery and Meaning of Christian Conversion* (Nashville: Discipleship Resources, 1981), pp. 53-57.

[6] Søren Kierkegaard, *Purity of Heart Is to Will One Thing: Spiritual Preparation for the Feast of Confession* (New York: Harper and Brothers, 1938), p. 69.

[7] Morris.

[8] John R. W. Stott, *Christian Mission in the Modern World* (Downers Grove, Ill: InterVarsity Press, 1975), pp. 21-22.

[9] Michael Green, *Evangelism in the Early Church* (Grand Rapids: Eerdmans, 1970), pp. 236ff.

[10] Ibid.

CHAPTER THREE

[1] John R. Hendrick, *Opening the Door of Faith* (Atlanta: John Knox Press, 1977).

[2] Morris.

[3] John Wesley, "Of True Christian Faith" in *John Wesley*, ed. Albert C. Outler (New York: Oxford University Press, 1964), p. 129.

[4] John Wesley, "Doctrinal Summaries" in *John Wesley*, ed. Albert C. Outler, p. 189.

[5] John Wesley, "Marks of the New Birth" in *Wesley's Doctrinal Standards, Part 1*, ed. N. Burwash (Salem, Ohio: Schmul Publishers, 1967 (Reprint), p. 174.

[6] John Wesley, "Justification by Faith" in *John Wesley*, ed. Albert C. Outler, p. 205.

[7] Paul Scherer, *The Word God Sent* (New York: Harper and Row, 1965), p. 6.

CHAPTER FOUR

[1] Morris.

[2] Thomas C. Oden, *Requiem: A Lament in Three Movements* (Nashville: Abingdon Press, 1995).

[3] Morris.

[4] John R. W. Stott, *Christian Mission in the Modern World*, pp. 27-41; and Leander E. Keck, *A Future for the Historical Jesus* (Nashville: Abingdon Press, 1971), pp. 100-153.

[5] Morris.

[6] Gabriel Fackre, *Word in Deed* (Grand Rapids: Eerdmans, 1975), pp. 52-77.

[7] Morris.

[8] Everett F. Harrison, "Romans" in *Expositor's Bible Commentary*, edited by Frank E. Gaebelein (Grand Rapids: Zondervan, 1976), p. 156.

[9] Morris.

CHAPTER FIVE

[1] Eugene Nida, *Message and Mission* (South Pasadena: William Carey Library, 1972), p. 58.

2 See Donald Soper, "The Setting for Making Christians Today," in *Rethinking Evangelism,* ed. by George G. Hunter III (Nashville: Discipleship Resources, 1978), pp. 18-28.

3 Kenneth Scott Latourette, *History of the Expansion of Christianity,* Vol. 1.

4 George G. Hunter III, *The Contagious Congregation* (Nashville: Abingdon, 1979), p. 40.

5 Bryan Green, *The Practice of Evangelism* (New York: Scribner's, 1951), pp. 77-84.

6 Hunter, p. 91.

7 "Religion in America, 50 Years, 1935-1985." The Gallup Report 236. (May 1985), p. 57.

8 Donald Soper, "The Setting for Making Christians Today," in *Rethinking Evangelism,* ed., George G. Hunter III (Nashville: Discipleship Resources, 1978), pp. 73-75.

9 Ibid.

10 Hunter, pp. 73-75

11 Hunter, pp. 96-97.

12 Fox.

13 Paul E. Little, *How to Give Away Your Faith* (Downer's Grove, Ill.: InterVarsity Press, 1966), pp. 83-91.

14 See Chester E. Custer, *All Things New* (Nashville: Tidings, 1972), pp. 20-29.

15 Keith Miller, *The Becomers* (Waco, Texas: Word Books, 1973), as quoted in Hunter, *The Contagious Congregation*, pp. 40-41.

16 Hunter, pp. 41-46.

17 Fox.

18 Donald McGavran, *Understanding Church Growth*, Revised Edition (Grand Rapids, Mich.: Eerdmans, 1980), pp. 245-265, and Hunter, *The Contagious Congregation*, pp. 104-128.

19 Win and Charles Arn, *The Master's Plan* (Pasadena, Calif.: Church Growth Press, 1982), p. 91.

20 George E. Morris, *The Mystery and Meaning of Christian Conversion* (Nashville: Discipleship Resources, 1984), p. 110.

CHAPTER SIX

1 Eugene Nida, *Message and Mission*, p. 162.

2 Fox.

CHAPTER SEVEN

1 *The Pastor's Church Growth Handbook II*, ed. Win Arn, The Institute for American Church Growth (Pasadena, Calif.: Church Growth Press), pp. 139-144.

2 *Church Growth: America* (Nov.-Dec., 1978 and Sept.-Oct., 1979).

3 Win Arn, *The Pastor's Manual for Effective Ministry* (Monrovia, Calif.: Church Growth Inc, 1990).

4 Win Arn, "Do You Know Your Extended Congregation?" in *Net Results*, edited by Herb Miller, Vol. XII, No. 4 (April 1991), p. 18.

5 Ibid.

6 Harold Rogers, *Harry Denman: A Biography* (Nashville: The Upper Room, 1977), p. 41.

7 As quoted in *Christianity Today*, Vol. 39, No. 3 (March 6, 1995), p. 41.

8 J. Russell Hale, *The Unchurched* (San Francisco: Harper and Row, 1954), pp. 182-184.

9 Rogers, p. 42.

10 Dietrich Bonhoeffer, *Life Together* (New York: Harper and Row, 1954), pp. 97-99.

11 Morris.

12 Richard Armstrong, *Service Evangelism* (Philadelphia: Westminster Press, 1979), pp. 93-94.

13 Morris.

14 Ibid.

15 See Fred Craddock, *Overhearing the Gospel* (Nashville: Abingdon Press, 1978) for a helpful description of Kierkegaard's method.

16 Lyle Schaller, *It's a Different World* (Nashville: Abingdon Press, 1987), pp. 215-217.

17 Kennon L. Callahan, *Twelve Keys to an Effective Church* (San Francisco: Harper and Row, 1983), pp. 39ff.

18 Ibid.

19 Morris.

20 Morris and Fox.

[21] Morris.

[22] Ibid.

[23] Fox.

[24] Morris.

CHAPTER EIGHT

[1] Bryan Green, "Counseling the Seeker" in *Focus on Evangelism*, edited by George G. Hunter III (Nashville: Discipleship Resources, 1978), p. 114.

[2] Ibid.

[3] Albert Outler, *Works of John Wesley* (Nashville: Abingdon Press, 1984), Vol. 1, p. 98.

[4] Ibid, p. 118.

[5] *The Works of Wesley* (Baker Book House, Third Edition), Vol. 1, p. 103.

[6] *Saved By Grace*. Statement adopted by the World Methodist Council, Nairobi, Kenya, 1986, printed by Discipleship Resources, Nashville, 1987.

[7] John Baillie, *Invitation to Pilgrimage* (London: Oxford University Press, 1942), p. 119.

[8] George E. Morris, *The Mystery and Meaning of Christian Conversion* (Nashville: Discipleship Resources, 1981), pp. 136-140.

[9] *The Works of the Rev. John Wesley*, 3rd ed., edited by Thomas Jackson (London: Wesleyan-Methodist Book Room, 1829-31), Vol. V, pp. 296, 302.

[10] Harold Rogers, *Harry Denman: A Biography*, p. 56.

CHAPTER NINE

[1] Mack B. Stokes, *The Holy Spirit* (Nashville: Abingdon Press, 1985), p. 9.

[2] Fox.

[3] Leander E. Keck, *Mandate to Witness* (Valley Forge, Pa: Judson Press, 1964), p. 52.

[4] Glenn "Tex" Evans, *Life Is Like That* (Nashville: Discipleship Resources, 1975), pp. 1-4.

[5] "There Is a Balm in Gilead," *The United Methodist Hymnal* (Nashville: United Methodist Publishing House, 1989), 375.

Bibliography

Abraham, William J. *The Logic of Evangelism*. Grand Rapids: William B. Eerdmans, 1989.

_____. *Waking from Doctrinal Amnesia*. Nashville: Abingdon Press, 1995.

Armstrong, Richard. *Service Evangelism*. Philadelphia: Westminster Press, 1979.

Arn, Win and Charles. *The Master's Plan*. Pasadena, Calif.: Church Growth Press, 1982.

Arn, Win, ed. *The Pastor's Church Growth Handbook*. The Institute for American Church Growth. Pasadena, Calif: Church Growth Press.

Baillie, John. *Invitation to Pilgrimage*. London: Oxford University Press, 1942.

Bonhoeffer, Dietrich. *Life Together*. New York: Harper and Row, 1954.

Callahan, Kennon L. *Twelve Keys to an Effective Church*. San Francisco: Harper and Row, 1983.

_____. *Visiting in an Age of Mission*. San Francisco: Harper, 1994.

Church Growth: America, November-December, 1978 and September-October, 1979, Institute for American Church Growth. Pasadena, Calif.: Church Growth Press.

Coleman, Robert E. *The Master Plan of Evangelism*. Grand Rapids: Fleming H. Revell, 1963.

Cowell, W. James. *Extending Your Congregation's Welcome*. Nashville: Discipleship Resources, 1989.

Custer, Chester E. *All Things New*. Nashville: Tidings, 1972.

DeWolf, L. Harold. *The Aim of Evangelism*. Nashville: Methodist Evangelistic Materials, 1965.

Dunnam, Maxie D. *Alive in Christ*. Nashville: Abingdon Press, 1982.

_____. *Going on to Salvation*. Nashville: Discipleship Resources, 1963.

_____. *This Is Christianity*. Nashville: Abingdon Press, 1994.

English, Donald. *Why Believe in Jesus?* London: Epworth Press, 1986.

Evans, Glenn "Tex." *Life Is Like That*. Nashville: Tidings, 1975.

Fackre, Gabriel. *Word in Deed*. Grand Rapids, Mich.: Eerdmans, 1975.

Fox and Morris. *Let the Redeemed of the Lord SAY SO!* Nashville: Abingdon Press, 1991.

_____. *The Faith-Sharing New Testament with Psalms*. Nashville: Abingdon Press, 1996.

Fox, H. Eddie. *Grace-Esteem*. Nashville: Discipleship Resources, 1988.

Ford, Leighton. *The Power of Story*. Colorado Springs: NavPress, 1994.

Gallup Report, Religion in America 50 Years, 1935–1985. Report No. 236. Princeton, N.J., May 1985.

Green, Bryan. "Counseling the Seeker," *Focus on Evangelism*, ed. George G. Hunter III. Nashville: Discipleship Resources, 1978.

_____. *The Practice of Evangelism*. New York: Scribner's, 1951.

Green, Michael. *Evangelism in the Early Church*. Grand Rapids: Eerdmans, 1970.

Hendrick, John R. *Opening the Door of Faith*. Atlanta: John Knox Press, 1977.

Hunter, George G. III. *The Contagious Congregation*. Nashville: Abingdon Press, 1979.

_____. *How to Reach Secular People*. Nashville: Abingdon Press, 1992.

_____. *To Spread the Power*. Nashville: Abingdon Press, 1987.

Jackson, Thomas, ed. *The Works of the Reverend John Wesley*, 3rd ed. London: Wesleyan-Methodist Book Room, 1829-31, Vol. 5.

Johnson, Ben. *Speaking of God*. Louisville: Westminster, 1991.

Johnson, Ronald W. *How Will They Hear if We Don't Listen?* Nashville: Broadman Press, 1994.

Keck, Leander E. *The Church Confident*. Nashville: Abingdon Press, 1993.

_____. *A Future for the Historical Jesus*. Nashville: Abingdon Press, 1971.

_____. *Mandate to Witness*. Valley Forge, Pa.: Judson Press, 1964.

Kierkegaard, Søren. *Purity of Heart Is to Will One Thing: Spiritual Preparation for the Feast of Confession*. New York: Harper and Brothers, 1938.

Little, Paul E. *How to Give Away Your Faith*. Downers Grove, Ill.: InterVarsity Press, 1966.

Luther, Martin. *Lectures on Romans* in *Luther's Works*. Vol. 25.

Mallison, John. *How to Become a Follower of Jesus Christ*. NSW, Australia, Renewal Publications.

Mead, Loren B. *The Once and Future Church*. Washington, D.C.: Alban Institute, Revised 1994.

_____. *Transforming Congregations for the Future*. Washington, D.C.: Alban Institute, 1994.

McGavran, Donald. *Understanding Church Growth*. Grand Rapids: Eerdmans, Revised Edition, 1980.

Miller, Keith. *The Becomers*. Waco, Texas: Word Books, 1973.

Morris, George E. *The Mystery and Meaning of Christian Conversion*. Nashville: Discipleship Resources, 1981.

Newbigin, Leslie. *Foolishness to the Greeks*. Grand Rapids: Eerdmans Publishing Company, 1986.

Newton, John. "Amazing Grace," *The Book of Hymns*. Nashville: Methodist Publishing House, 1964.

Nida, Eugene. *Message and Mission*. South Pasadena, Calif.: William Carey Library, 1972.

Oden, Thomas C. *Requiem*. Nashville: Abingdon Press, 1995.

Outler, Albert. *The Works of Wesley*. Nashville: Abingdon Press, 1984.

Rogers, Harold. *Harry Denman: A Biography*. Nashville: The Upper Room, 1977.

Scherer, Paul. *The Word God Sent*. New York: Harper and Row, 1965.

Soper, Donald. "The Setting for Making Christians Today," *Rethinking Evangelism*, ed. George G. Hunter III. Nashville: Discipleship Resources, 1978.

Stokes, Mack B. *The Holy Spirit*. Nashville: Abingdon Press, 1985.

Storey, Peter. *The Kingdom People*. Nashville: Discipleship Resources, 1984.

Stott, John R. W. *Christian Mission in the Modern World*. Downers Grove, Ill.: InterVarsity Press, 1975.

Snyder, Howard. *The Radical Wesley*. Downer's Grove, Ill.: InterVarsity Press, 1980.

Thompson, Francis. "The Hound of Heaven." 1893.

Walker, Alan. *The New Evangelism*. Nashville: Abingdon Press, 1975.

Wesley, John. "Doctrinal Summaries," *John Wesley*, ed. Albert C. Outler. New York: Oxford University Press, 1964.

_____. "Justification by Faith," *John Wesley*, ed. Albert C. Outler.

_____. "Marks of the New Birth," *Wesley's Doctrinal Standards, Part 1*, ed. N. Burwash. Salem, Ohio: Schmul Publishers, 1967.

Wagner, C. Peter. *Churches That Pray*. Ventura, Calif.: Regal Books, 1993.

Wood, A. Skevington. *The Burning Heart*. Minneapolis: Bethany Fellowship, 1978.

Recommended Reading

Articles about evangelism and information about programs are available on the Evangelism page of the General Board of Discipleship website (http://www.gbod.org/evangelism).

Arias, Mortimer. *Announcing the Reign of God.* Philadelphia: Fortress Press, 1984.

Coleman, Robert. *The Master Plan of Evangelism.* Grand Rapids: Fleming H. Revell, 1993.

Faith-Sharing Video Kit. Nashville: Discipleship Resources, 1996.

Gebhard, Duane M. *The Growing Points Star: A Tool for Disciple Formation.* Nashville: Discipleship Resources, 2000.

Harrington, Peter. *10 FAQ's of New Christians.* Nashville: Discipleship Resources, 2000.

Johnson, Ben. *An Evangelism Primer: Practical Principles for Congregations.* Atlanta: Westminster John Knox Press, 1983.

Mercer, Jerry L. *Living Deeply Our New Life in Christ: A Wesleyan Spirituality for Today.* Nashville: Discipleship Resources, 1999.

Metzger, Will. *Tell the Truth.* Downers Grove, Ill.: InterVarsity Press, 1981.

Miller, Craig Kennet. *NextChurch.Now: Creating New Faith Communities.* Nashville: Discipleship Resources, 2000.

Nouwen, Henri J. M. *Reaching Out.* Garden City, N.Y.: Image, 1986.

Outler, Albert C. *Evangelism and Theology in the Wesleyan Spirit.* Nashville: Discipleship Resources, 1996.

Packer, J. L. *Evangelism and the Sovereignty of God* (Second Edition). Downers Grove, Ill.: InterVarsity Press, 2001.

Personal FRAN Plan. Nashville: Discipleship Resources, 1998.

Pippert, Rebecca Manley. *Out of the Saltshaker and into the World: Evangelism as a Way of Life.* Downers Grove, Ill.: InterVarsity Press, revised and expanded 1999.

Swanson, Roger K. and Clement, Shirley F. *The Faith-Sharing Congregation.* Nashville: Discipleship Resources, 1996.

Westerhoff, John III. *Will Our Children Have Faith?* (Revised Edition). Harrisburg, Pa.: Morehouse Publishing Co., 2000.

Willimon, William H. *The Gospel for the Person Who Has Everything.* Valley Forge, Pa.: Judson Press, 1978.